Strategic Learning and Leading Change

T0300051

New Frontiers in Learning

The **New Frontiers in Learning Series** features books presenting cutting edge developments in learning practices that drive performance in organizations. Particular attention is given to strategically focused linkages between learning and performance. However, the focal point of each book in the series is on learning processes and performance outcomes at the individual, team, and/or organizational level. The theme that unifies the books in the series is learning solutions that add value in highly competitive environments, including both the non-profit and for-profit sectors.

Titles in the series:

STRATEGIC LEARNING AND LEADING CHANGE

How Global Organizations are Reinventing HR

Stephen John

LONDON AND NEW YORK

First published by Butterworth-Heinemann

First edition 2009

This edition published 2011 by Routledge
2 Park Square, Milton Park, Abingdon, Oxon, OX14 4RN
711 Third Avenue, New York, NY 10017, USA

Routledge is an imprint of the Taylor & Francis Group, an informa business

Copyright © 2009 Taylor & Francis. All rights reserved

Notice
No responsibility is assumed by the publisher for any injury and/or damage to persons or property as a matter of products liability, negligence or otherwise, or from any use or operation of any methods, products, instructions or ideas contained in the material herein

Library of Congress Cataloging-in-Publication Data
A catalogue record for this book is available from the Library of Congress

British Library Cataloguing-in-Publication Data
A catalogue record for this book is available from the British Library

ISBN: 978-0-7506-8288-6
ISSN: 1876-1852

To my wife Dona and my daughter Stacy and
My Mother Nellie and Father George

To Dream the Impossible Dream
To Go Where Others Dare Not Go

    – From Soundtrack-Man of LaMancha

Contents

Foreword

"Strategic learning is about understanding the global strategy and how each part of the organization, wherever it is located, contributes their best, most innovative thinking followed up by actions that execute the strategic intent of the organization".

Steve begins this book with the best definition of organizational learning that I have ever encountered. It begins with the recognition of need for a truly *global* strategy — not just an international strategy that really revolves around the home country. He continues on to recognize the need for *each* part of the organization to make their best contribution — not just compliance to top management. He finishes with the importance of *actions* that actually execute the strategic intent — not attendance at programs where the goal is to provide a few "a-ha" moments to participants.

Globalization is an ongoing trend that will eventually impact the way that everyone on our planet does business. Companies that embrace globalization will have challenges — but will have a fighting chance to survive in the new world. Companies that do not will probably die.

This book is even more important for corporations in the "developed" world, than it is for companies in the "developing" world.

Tom Brokaw's book, *The Greatest Generation*, praises the achievements of my parents' age group in the United States. While I love the USA, I think that this generation was far more "lucky" than "great".

I was brought up in Valley Station, Kentucky. When I recently went back for my fortieth high-school reunion, a conversation with my friend Mary illustrated how the world had changed — and why this book is so important.

Mary talked about her Dad, Bob. Bob was poorly educated, never tried very hard in school and had an extremely poor work ethic. He got a job in a factory — which was pretty easy to do at the time — was in a union — and was almost impossible to fire. He called in sick whenever he could and did the minimum about of work required to keep his assembly line job. Bob did absolutely nothing to educate himself during his working career. He put in 30 years at the plant, retired in his 50s, and had lifetime health care and pension benefits (which he collected for over 30 years and his wife is still collecting). He lived in a small, but nice house in the suburbs. His wife did not work and he raised three children — who all graduated from college.

Mary went on to contrast her Dad, Bob's life with the life of her son, Jason. She talked about how hard Jason worked (60 hours per week) and how little money he made. Jason, at age 24, was still living at home to save money. If he had to pay rent on an apartment, he could save almost nothing. He had finished three years of college and was facing student loan bills. Jason faced a future where it was highly unlikely that he would ever match the lifestyle of his grandfather, Bob.

Bob was not great. Bob was lucky. In his days, almost any white male who was born in the United States could live a middle-class lifestyle. Those days are over! The world has changed.

I travel constantly and am amazed at what I see around the world. Millions of highly educated people from developing countries speak fluent English and are willing to work very hard. Bob did not have to compete with any of these people, but Jason does. Bob could "coast" through life, but Jason cannot.

The example of Bob and Jason is being lived out throughout the developed world. In Italy hundreds of thousands of 35+ year-old men are still living with Mom and Dad. In Japan, a new generation has seen almost no growth for years. In Germany, a coming demographic quake is going to upset their cherished social structure.

Welcome to the new world!

Just as the world has changed for individuals, it has changed for corporations.

Steve mentions IBM as a case study. As a consultant, IBM was my largest client in the late 1970s and early 1980s. In those days, at IBM headquarters, you could have fired a cannon ball down the hall at 5 PM and hit no one. Almost all of the employees worked only 40 hours per week and took 4–5 week vacations. They had no real competitors. The same applied to AT&T, Kodak, Xerox, and many other large Western corporations. They could afford to have millions of employees like Bob!

Those days are over.

In the same way that professionals in the West need more education than ever before — and work harder than ever before — corporations will be challenged to be better than ever before — just to keep up!

In the "old days" IBM was considered to have about the best training in the world. How did they measure results? By how many hours participants sat in classes and how popular the training programs were.

These were very stupid measures then — and are ridiculous measures now.

In *Strategic Learning and Leading Change*, Steve is providing a playbook for the organizations of the future. As he notes, learning will not be about participants sitting in rooms, laughing at funny stories, evaluating instructors, and commenting on the quality of lunch. Learning will be about making a real difference and facilitating the execution of the corporation's global strategy.

In the same way that employees are changing and companies are changing, learning methodologies are going to change. Organizational learning will be about producing results. It will be "real" and focus on impact. It will be designed for the World — not just the West. And it will be dynamic.

As you read on, think about your own organization and your own life. Be willing to apply what you learn as soon as you can!

While the new world, with global competition, changing labor force and the need for cross-cultural understanding is more challenging than ever before — it can also be more exciting!

Apply everything that you learn in this book to make a positive difference for yourself, your company, and our world.

Marshall Goldsmith
Ranch Sante Fe, California
June 2008

Preface

Don Quixote, since its publishing in 1604 by Cervantes, has captured the fancy and imaginations of people all over the world and of all ages. Each of us can identify with Quixote or with his side kick Sancho Panza's view of reality and sometimes we see both in ourselves. Quixote sees alternatives where others, including Sancho, see only the facts sordid as they are. Cervantes, well before multinational corporations roamed the landscape, successfully captured life's paradoxes. Each of us experiences the paradox of reality or illusion as we make our way through the world. Sancho throughout the quest tries to bring Quixote back to reality. Don Quixote sees a different world. He sees a world where people should act with kindness to others and always out of the courage of their convictions.

Don Quixote tells us late in story the goal of the knight-errant must be to "explore the most hidden recesses of the universe, plunge into the perplexities of the labyrinth, and not be afraid of even impossibilities". Sound advice, over 400 years later, for those of us working to build global business organizations. Organizations today must be high performing and also provide cultures that engage their employee's passions. Like Quixote, we can choose to see the alternatives that are mired by the facts or we can act like Sancho seeing the facts and accepting the world as it is. It is a reality that there are more organizations in the world that do not ignite peoples passions nor do they embrace strategic learning and with courage, lead the necessary change. My quest, over the last two decades, has been to understand how strategic learning shows up in global organizations or not and how change can be facilitated from the lesson learned or not. When organizations practice strategic learning and then use it to lead change, we find organizations that are all about possibilities and the facts are used, as they should be, to support strategic learning and lead change. These organizations have cultures that people deeply connect to just as Sancho became inseparable from Don Quixote. He could not help himself. He was drawn to the light. In the movie version staring Peter O'Toole, Sancho gets it at the end. He understands there is reality but there is also possibility. The best of both worlds comes together in strategic learning and leading change.

Improving strategy execution is at the top of everyone's list — senior business leaders, shareholders, and stakeholders. Companies of all sizes, all geographies, and across all industries are struggling to increase their capability in strategy formulation and communication, alignment of employees goals and activities, increasing innovation, shortening cycle times such as time from discovery to market, lowering operating costs without decrease in quality, and engaging employees at all levels in the mission, vision, and values of the organization. For some companies, the globalization of their industry and hence their company is at the top of their challenges list.

Global organizations that aspire to long-term sustainability must master both strategic learning and leading change. Every organization in the world that is global, in the process of going global or thinking about globalizing itself must prepare itself for continuous culture changes that will, in many cases, shake its identity, i.e. its very core beliefs and values. Pharmaceutical companies for decades discovered and commercialized their products with a country strategy and not a global strategy. These same companies now must form global teams with every kind of diversity imaginable represented on the team. Team members have different technical specialties, national cultures, generational differences, gender differences, race, and work and life experiences. This reality can become a strength of the organization or it can bring fragmentation to its identity.

Strategic learning is about understanding the global strategy and how each part of the organization, wherever it is located, contributes their best, most innovative thinking followed up by actions that execute the strategic intent of the organization. The organization recognizes the paradoxes presented by globalization and does not rest until an innovative, low cost, high-quality solution is provided. These organizations depend on team-based learning that expects that after a team creates new knowledge, it shares it with the larger organization. Strategy, structure, processes, and culture all need to be working together to accomplish this effectively. Strategic learning identifies the areas of alignment and misalignment as well. Strategic learning provides the blueprint or roadmap for every employee to step up and lead the necessary changes to strategy, structure, process, and/or culture.

Leading any cultural change, under the best of circumstances, is never easy. To do so when the organization must also become a strategic learning machine capable of conceptualizing and then delivering a continuous stream of product and/or service innovations to its customers may appear to be an impossible dream. These innovations must be flawlessly delivered. Sony did not have to turn on its television sets after manufacture because six sigma teams had built in quality before they were manufactured. Their operating processes were executed with flawless precision.

Today's consumer expects everything they purchase to work right the first time and to last without repair until they are ready to replace it. Most replacements are now based not on obsolescence but on the consumer being enticed to purchase the next generation product that has an innovative feature that appeals to them. The 21st century imperative for global business is to deliver these innovations through global teams that must frequently work virtually. Often, it is not possible to have more than one face-to-face meeting to start the team off. The team most likely will be larger than sound theory tells us it should be: 10–20 people — of different nationalities, technical specialties, multiple generations, gender, and races. Every conceivable difference will most likely be represented on the team. A number of them will be in time zones where daily or weekly verbal or video-based meetings will be impossible. Work will have to be split up into groups where team members may also be dispersed across time zones or geographies.

This demands a sense of urgency, a willingness to communicate openly and concisely, and trust that the organization's performance and rewards and talent management strategies and processes will recognize their individual contribution and that career progression will be based on merit and not political favoritism. Employees must also trust in the leadership of their organization, in their capability to set strategy and execute flawlessly, and to identify team member contributions and reward appropriately. Finally, when cultures need to be changed, we must all have the courage to lead the way.

Structure of this book

This book is structured into three Parts. Part I discusses the globalization of businesses and its impact on their strategy, structure, operations, and culture. Part II looks at APC, a European-based Pharma company, that was determined to reinvent their industries business model by building a global team-based organization that would deliver innovative drugs to patients in 6–9 years as opposed to the 12 plus years that has been the industry standard. This would be a 50 percent reduction in the cycle time from molecule discovery to patient usage. They would accomplish this by embedding strategic learning and culture change capability throughout their organization. Global HR as well as functional and country HR within APC was expected to lead the way and to be role models for the business functions. Part III examines the role of HR in today's business environment. Many business leaders have little faith in HR to deliver anything but administrative services. By many accounts an HR department is in a crisis situation fighting for its survival as an internal function within their company. As Human Resource Outsourcing becomes more effective and efficient HR departments become more vulnerable and in danger of going the way of the "buggy whip" after automobiles were invented. This Part makes the case for reinventing HR. It is too late to reengineer it. The pessimism about HRs value added to an organization's strategy execution efforts can only be turned into optimism by reinvention.

Part I: The Globalization of Business

Chapter 1 discusses the phenomenon of globalization and its impact on companies. Companies of all sizes, large and small, domestic and international, across all industry. Sectors have had — over the past 10–15 years — to rethink their strategies and operations and in some cases their very core beliefs and identity. The changes to their respective industry and their place in it frequently came fast and furiously — leaving little time to carefully plan a detailed change process. Learning and the ensuing change had to be handled on the run. This chapter is an overview of the globalization phenomena from the perspective of economic, social, and governmental forces and how they converged to cause both chaos and complexity in many organizations. The impact of globalization on IBM and General Electric are explored for lessons learned.

Chapter 2 explores the challenges that leaders and managers face in building global organizations. Companies that have globalized either voluntarily or through external marketplace forces have also experienced significant strain on their performance management, talent management, and leadership development strategies and practices. Leaders and managers in a globalizing organization face issues that must be quickly resolved around: (1) strategy and structure, (2) cross-cultural cooperation, and (3) people's roles, accountabilities, and rewards. These three areas must be aligned at the global level and operationalized locally in order for an organization to successfully execute its strategy. A case is examined for the above issues illustrating how a Pharma company handled these challenges when they decided to outsource clinical trials. Clinical trials have, historically, been a core competence of a Pharma company and the decision to outsource brought chaos and fear to employees throughout the organization. The role of strategic learning is explored and how it can be utilized to mitigate the challenges that surface when an organization makes major changes to its strategic direction.

Chapter 3 discusses the role of teams as a core part of a global strategy including the shift in mind-set and cross-cultural capabilities needed by leaders and members of global teams will also be discussed. Strategic learning is defined and how it impacts culture as well as how culture impacts strategic learning. The critical role that senior leadership/management plays in coaching the organization's top talents for peak performance in the current business cycle as well as accelerating their growth for their career growth is explored. Leading change and in particular culture change is discussed and the use of Social Network Analysis is introduced as a promising technology that when intertwined with strategic learning is a powerful way to successfully lead culture change in the most resistant organizations. LVMH and Lonza are presented as examples of companies in two very different industries and how they utilized strategic learning and leading change concepts to successfully transform their companies.

Part II: Reinventing Pharma

The Pharma industry historically enjoyed very high margins in spite of the risks associated with bringing a molecule to product launch. The timeline from discovery to a sale is in the

10–15 year range. Many things can change over that time period: the competition can successfully launch a superior product, the disease can be treated using different modalities than using a prescription drug, and/or healthcare agencies/ governmental departments no longer cover the cost of the drug, and so on. Additional forces such as shorter patent protection periods, generic competition, efficacy and safety concerns surface, e.g. vioxx, and drug innovation declines and hence productivity with lots of "me too" drugs entering the marketplace, e.g. statins such as Lipitor and Crestor doing the exact same thing to lower cholesterol. These forces and others converged in the 1990s with the resulting change in thinking by some pharma executives about the viability of employing a country-based strategy to develop and launch blockbuster level drugs. Blockbuster drugs are defined by most in the industry to have sales per year greater than 1 billion dollars. While most pharma executives agreed that the country-based strategy had outlived its usefulness there was little agreement on what strategy should take its place. Some executives felt that a globally coordinated strategy would be the one to move to. This could take various forms in practice. Several of these alternate forms will be explored before turning to the APC way of globalizing Pharma.

APC (a European-based Pharma) was fortunate indeed. Since its formation in late 1999 from two medium-sized, mediocre-performing pharma companies, it had an aura of excitement and mystery about it. Recruiting new talent into the organization, while challenging because of the sheer number of people needed, was not especially difficult. There was lots of buzz about APC both internally as well as externally about this new kind of Pharma Company and how it intended to globalize the pharma business. Existing employees unashamedly talked about the excitement they felt in being part of a new kind of Pharma Company. A company that was truly global in its strategy, vision, and operating processes. APC employees prided themselves on creating a Global high performing teams (GHPT)-based organization — not using teams as a way to execute strategy, but global teams were the strategy. Of course the highly competitive nature of the modern pharma landscape required that these teams be nothing less than high performing. Everyone in APC knew it would be difficult to "pull off".

Chapter 4 explores the APC approach to globalizing their strategy and structure. The Executive Committee (EC), from the very beginning, designed a reporting structure that would ensure effective strategy execution. The EC consisted of the Chairman/CEO and his direct reports. Only global function heads reported to the CEO. The intent was to develop a clear strategy and its execution would be at the global level and not at the country head/General Manager level as in many other Pharma companies. Specifically the global functions were: Commercial Operations, Industrial Operations, R&D, HR, IT, Communications, Legal, Finance, and Strategic Alliances. These functions covered all key areas needed to effectively plan, communicate, and execute strategy. Country Heads reported to a global function head. In addition to global functional reporting relationships, the EC assigned global budget as well as profit and loss (P&L) responsibility to the global function heads that in turn assigned similar responsibilities to their global product teams (GPT).

Each global function head was expected to build high-performance global teams within their respective functions as well as across functions. The mandate was clear. Global teams within a function and then across functions were the core of the APC strategy. Specifically the Commercial, Industrial, and R&D functions would set shared cross-functional goals at the global function head level and then cascade them to their direct reports who in turn would cascade them to their direct reports and so on down through the organization. Most cross-functional goal setting at each level would take place in face-to-face meetings which required a great deal of travel for team members. Meeting locations would be held in different countries so that all participants would be equally traveling to ensure fairness.

Shared global goals across the functions would not be sufficient to make APC's vision of a global pharma company a reality. APC had hundreds of products sold in a large number of countries. APC would have to change that quickly. The EC adopted a strategic brand focus to complement the GHPT concept. This focus emphasized discovering and launching innovative drugs in therapeutic areas with high medical needs and large patient populations. A long-term goal was to have a number of these innovative products — a portfolio approach — for each of the disease group areas that APC was determined to be a major player in. APC went on to define more specifically what a strategic brand meant in terms of sales dollars and sales presence, i.e. countries. A yearly sale of 1 billion dollars with presence in the 12 core countries was their goal. Each product was reviewed to make a determination if it fit the strategic brand concept going forward. Those products not fitting the definition were sold to other companies where possible or discontinued.

The EC realized early on that globalizing the HR function was critical to their success in creating their global pharma company. In fact, HR would have to get global at least one step ahead of all the other functions if they were to succeed over the short term. It would also be impossible to sustain the global organization over the long term without the support of the HR function. It was the EC that early on embraced the Global Head of HR as a strategic business partner and coach. HR would play a key role integrating strategic learning with the key initiatives that needed to be accomplished by the global functions as well as the regional part of the organization. It would be internal HR consultants who would be the catalyst for the R&D function to link their strategy, processes, and people with specific strategic learning tools.

Throughout Chapters 5, 6, and 7 a diabetes drug (DD1302) is discussed to provide a specific context for discussing the strategic learning and change leadership challenges that APC faced as it implemented its global strategy.

Chapter 5 explores the APC approach to globalizing its R&D function. R&D would need to develop a unique set of learning strategies, tools, and processes to meet its needs. Employees in and out of the R&D function would need to understand the new paradigm and its impact on their work. They would need to align their goals and activities as well as their hearts to the new order of things. They were expected to bring to patients an innovative drug in a significantly shorter time period than the standard industry practice. Out of the fog of integration, it became clear that HR would be an important strategic player and that the speed and quality with which HR could transform itself would be one of the critical success factors for APC to meet its globalization challenge.

The APC strategy was clear — to deliver two or three significant new drug approvals per year. To achieve this, each function in APC would have to reduce their cycle time, increase innovation, and productivity. Pharma companies traditionally have separate functions for the research teams that discover the drugs and for the teams that develop the drug into a product that is ready to be marketed and sold to the physician and used by the patient. R&D was the APC answer to improving innovation and productivity. APC combined the research and development functions into one function — R&D. This combination was more than cosmetic or superficial. As one executive stated, "There are thousands of us with different specialties ... we have to find new ways of working together as well as learning from each other and spreading the wealth [strategic learnings] quickly and effectively throughout the place". It became very clear very quickly that a change in mind-set would have to occur at the individual, team, and functional level if R&D was to succeed in accomplishing its strategic goals. A team-based network centric versus hierarchical command and control top-down organization would have to be designed and deployed. R&D needed creative out of the box innovations to become the rule rather than the exception in the day-to-day strategy execution. The project teams became the basic unit of innovation. Each new potential drug had a project team assigned to it from discovery to the approval of the drug for sale. These project teams generated enormous amounts of data which in turn had to be converted into knowledge which then had to be shared with other teams in the R&D function and then with the organization at large. In addition, other functional areas, e.g. manufacturing, marketing, sales, legal, and communications also had to be aware of the strategic learnings in order to avoid reinventing the wheel if two or three new approvals per year were to be achieved.

The R&D strategy would need to be well formulated, communicated, and understood/aligned at the individual, team, and functional levels to be successfully implemented. The R&D leadership team (R&DLT) was accountable for this and would organize the function in such a way as to encourage high levels of innovation. Strategic learning (SL) would be a key part of the R&D culture. The R&D way will be defined starting with the design of the function, the "one page strategy" model of gaining quick understanding and support for the overall R&D strategy and the one page strategy for the project team. The project teams then had a number of learning tools and processes available to them based upon their specific need to achieve their goals. The global structure with linkages to the local sites and disease groups will be discussed as providing an understandable infrastructure to enable the flow of data, knowledge creation, and sharing/learning. Since networking, teamwork, and collaboration were essential to the functions successes, a number of knowledge/learning-based initiatives/tools were designed and deployed, e.g. Communities of Practice, high-performance team process, knowledge expertise locator, and recognition programs such as Champions of Knowledge Sharing.

Chapter 6 discusses the ECs concerns and approach to developing its current and future leadership talent. They agreed that in the first year of the integration there would be little time to send people to traditional leadership development programs or customize one for the new organization. Everyone was working way too hard to spend time in this area. The EC knew it also could not completely ignore the development of their leadership talent especially their high-potential talent. People would leave the organization if their development was ignored. As a result the EC working with HR leadership and an outside consultancy came up with an interim leadership development plan that fit the organization's needs until a more formal one could be designed and agreed to. All EC sponsored leadership Learning and Development (LD) was at the global level with all functions expecting to send participants identified in their Talent Management meetings — First, leadership development would be embedded into their yearly meeting of the Top 200. Well-known external business leaders would be brought in to work with the group in building awareness and skill in selected areas. For example, Jack Welch was brought in to discuss creating the boundaryless organization and differentiating performance and rewards.

The EC, with full support from global HR, used the year 2000 to their advantage as HR prepared itself for the challenges ahead. The CEO started the integration off with a meeting of the Top 200 business leaders across the organization that focused on identifying the critical issues APC faced with particular emphasis on the new company's values and the global teaming concept. As a result of the meeting a number of action learning teams (ALTs) were formed around the issues. These issues needed immediate solutions if APC was to successfully execute its strategy. Each ALT team would have an external coach who would provide in team just-in-time leadership development based on the needs of the team as they were executing their mandate. The timeline was quite short — in fact most employees described it as very aggressive but necessary. You could feel the passion in their voices as they described their teams, the work they did, and the results they achieved.

The ALTs were critical in rapidly moving APC to discuss and agree on strategies, shared terminology, processes, and policies around performance management, rewards, leadership development, and talent management. These teams were also critical in defining the global team-based organization.

In parallel to the above development activities, HR worked on designing a leadership success profile (ALP) specific to the new organization. This profile would become the foundation of the Talent Management, Performance Management, and Leadership Development strategies as APC moved rapidly to transform itself. A 360-degree assessment tool was designed after the senior leadership of the organization approved the profile. The EC then underwent a 360 assessment, debriefed by an outside coach, and made commitments to each other as part of their working meeting as to their individual development plans. The ECs commitment to the ALP profile, developing leadership skills critical to APC, and most importantly the transparency with which they did their 360 and then shared development plans went quickly throughout the organization. R&D HR working with Global HR quickly developed a business simulation and working with two leading Universities built and deployed a global business leader program. The chapter ends with a discussion of the Community of Practice around change leadership that formed out of the global business leader program and its substantial impact on APC's strategy execution efforts.

Chapter 7 explores the culture change APC needed to successfully implement its global team-based strategy. APC R&D was selected by the EC to take the lead on the culture change initiative. Two areas of the culture needed to be changed immediately if APC was to improve its market capitalization. The first area was sense of urgency/speed of execution and the second, networking, i.e. the capability of everyone in APC to strategically learn from each other across functions and geographies and then share their learning's across the organization. APC was number 5 in its industry in sales but only number 15 in market capitalization defined as number of shares of APC stock X the share price on the stock exchange. There were reservations by the financial analysts as well as institutional buyers such as large pension funds that

APC could deliver on its promise of building a global team-based organization and reducing cycle time from 12 years to 6 years. Their efforts in defining the culture change needed and then building acceptance across the organization are explored.

Part III: How Global Companies are Reinventing Human Resources

Chapter 8 explores how global companies are reinventing HR to gain sustainable competitive advantage in their industry. The disconnection between what HR thinks and then does to support their organization in executing its strategy are discussed. Several company examples are provided to identify the techniques these companies are utilizing to earn their seat at the EC table. A 100-day reinventing HR change plan is discussed which if implemented effectively can assist HR in regaining its reputation. HR can be the defining difference between an organization that successfully globalizes and those that do not. To achieve this distinction, it must reinvent itself and it must do so at the same speed many organizations have to make drastic changes to their strategic direction. If HR does not accept this challenge and reinvent itself, it most likely will go the way of the dinosaur. Organizations will globalize more slowly if at all, products available from these global organizations will not be as readily available throughout the world and career opportunities will be more limited to a person's geographic location. Consumers, stockholders, and employees will all share in the loss if HR does not accept the challenge of being the catalyst for the globalization of business and the resulting culture changes needed for success.

Senior Editor's Preface

The *Frontiers in Learning Series* was initiated for the purpose of presenting cutting edge learning practices for driving performance in organizations. In practice this meant paying particular attention to strategically focused linkages between learning and performance — looking at learning processes and practices that are critical for dealing with contexts and environments that are dynamic and complex. It has become commonplace to acknowledge that organizations have to function in contexts that are highly unpredictable and characterized by innovation. Strategic learning and adaptive leadership are widely accepted as critical competencies for managers and executives. Cultivating a learning organization is now a widely stated intention, if often an unrealized one. Thanks to the increasing pace of globalization and technological innovation, for many organizations learning at the individual, team, and organizational levels is no longer a source of competitive advantage, it is critical for survival.

That being said, positioning learning as a continuous process is increasingly challenging. The same dynamics that make learning an imperative also create pressures that tend to drive time for learning, at least in terms of traditional delivery systems, out of the organization. Informal, Incidental, Project or Work-Based Learning, are increasingly used terms in conversations learning in organizations. So too is the web, increasingly used to establish communities of practice and to connect social networks. Another consequence of the increasing rate of change and dynamism is a task-focused environment that creates the need for strategically positioning learning. Strategic learning itself is part of the capacity challenge facing organizations.

The literatures conceptualizing and studying the learning challenges implied by the above is growing and vast. At the same time the gap between research and practice is widening. As this is being written the issue of the engaged researcher and the value of academic and practitioner co-inquiry is a theme of debate in the upcoming Academy of Management Meetings. The contributors to this series have all done scholarly work, while applying to and learning lessons from practice. The inaugural book in this series, Julia Sloan's *Learning to Think Strategically* examines how executives widely regarded as having responsibility and capacity for strategic thinking developed their capabilities. Beginning with a foundation in the classic strategy literature Julia systemically studied how these individual's learned over time to develop their competencies in strategic thinking. Implications for practice and research are presented, implications Julia uses in her own practice. Terry Maltbia and Ann Powers book, *A Leaders Guide to Leveraging Diversity*, provides a practical framework, based on research, on how diversity is a strategic asset from a learning perspective. Their work provides an avenue for putting into practice the evidence that demonstrates that diversity is critical to innovation.

This volume by Stephen John *Strategic Learning and Leading Change: How Global Organizations are Reinventing HR*, shares the experiences of an organization seeking to strategically reposition itself, engage in organizational learning, and derive implications for developing people all to enhance performance. In the process, the organization was acquired resulting in more change. These are the lessons learned by a human resource executive, a learning professional who lived the journey, boots on the ground as the saying goes, and his implications for practice. As such, *Strategic Learning and Leading Change* makes a valuable contribution to both this series and the learning literature.

Acknowledgments

Every book is unique as is the process of creating it. For every author there are many people who are instrumental to the book coming to life and print. That said I alone accept responsibility for the quality of this book.

Thanks to my co-editors Carol Gorelick and Lyle Yorks and to Dennis McGonagle of Butterworth-Heinemann. My daughter Stacy keyed the manuscript and kept my spirits up as the deadline loomed. Ang Tarabokija lent her expertise in designing the Figures, formatting, and teaching me some of the technology nuances so necessary to produce a quality manuscript.

Michelle Limantour, a trusted colleague and dear friend, in spite of an overwhelming work schedule, found time to provide feedback and shared her insights in her cheerful way. Anika Gakovic was also instrumental in providing feedback and encouraging my spirit — a true friend. Anika gives me hope that the newest generation of HR professionals will positively impact the reputation of HR. Amy Bladden has been a source of energy and inspiration in sharing her love of working with organizations in times of difficult change. Michelle, Anika, and Amy are all committed to the socially responsible organization and work tirelessly to ensure it becomes a reality.

Many have enabled my strategic learning and leading change journey. Jim Minogue has been a constant source of inspiration. He is the best example of earning a seat at the table well over a decade before it became fashionable to discuss. If every HR function had a Jim, there would not be a "Why We Hate HR" article written. Anita Shendalman also earned a seat at the table for globalization of APC. Without her influence and ability to apply her HR expertise, APC would never have gotten off the ground in building its global team-based organization. A number of other professionals and friends have played a prominent part in my life. Francine Deutsch, Jo Singel, Alvin Piket, Josette Jean-Francois, Pat Santen, Patricia Murphy, Keith Mullin, Bill Keller, and Antoine Gerschel. I hold all of them dear to my heart. Special thanks to my friend and colleague Bob Schachet who passed away much too early in life.

Finally, my thanks to Uncle Mike Lefanto, who over 30 years ago saw things in me that I did not see in myself. I would not be writing this book if he had not taken an interest in me and mentored me.

THE GLOBALIZATION OF BUSINESS

Part I discusses the globalization of businesses and its impact on their strategy, structure, operating processes, and culture. Chapter 1 explores the history of globalization. Some companies have had to rethink their strategies and operations as well as their identity and core beliefs. IBM and GE Medical Systems are discussed as examples of how leadership proactively solves globalization challenges as they execute their strategy. Chapter 2 discusses, primarily through a Pharma Outsourcing case study, how leaders and managers respond to the challenges presented to them in their performance management, leadership development, and talent management philosophies and processes in a global business environment. Chapter 3 explores the role of teams and the cross-cultural capabilities needed in executing a global strategy. The eight principles of strategic learning are discussed in the context of performance and development coaching skills needed by leaders/managers of global organizations. Also covered is the use of Social Network Analysis and community building as major change implementation tools. LVMH and Lonza are presented as examples of diverse organizations successfully using strategic learning and leading change techniques to transform their organizations.

Enter Globalization

Globalization has arrived in the world, but not in most of the world's organizations.

Rhinesmith (1996)

A little over a decade later, there are more questions and challenges for leaders of today's business organizations. The media displays a wide array of contradictory images in portraying the globalization of business. We see business leaders, politicians, and Hollywood celebrities toasting globalization at the World Economic Summit held each year in Davos, Switzerland. We saw riots in the streets of Seattle with ensuing property damage when the WTO held its conference there several years ago.

Companies of all sizes — large and small, domestic and international — across all industries have had to rethink their strategic intent, operations, and in some cases their core beliefs and values. Leaders and employees in many organizations are challenging their identity, their purpose, and some argue their soul. As the French so eloquently say raison d'être.

Organizational Identity

An organization's identity is an important factor in how they define their value proposition to their customers in the marketplace and as importantly their value proposition to their employees who create and deliver on the organization's strategic intent. The degree of clarity the leadership communicates by words and actions impacts, positively or negatively, the depth of passion and zeal with which the organization's employees deliver on its value proposition to customers. Identity as it shapes leadership and management philosophy within an organization becomes a prime force in shaping and reshaping the culture. This can be especially true for organizations facing rapid changes and shifts within their industry as well as the forces due to merger and integration activities. Identity can be lost and regained and lost again and emerge as very different from the original identity. These changes can be extremely disorienting to the leadership and employees alike. Globalization can exacerbate an already turbulent environment. As we will see later, strategic learning and leading change is a 21st-century mandate for everyone in the organization. They must become woven into the very identity and behaviors of every individual in the organization to ensure its long-term sustainability.

The power of identity for positive or negative impact on an organization is best seen when the leaders chose to shape the identity of their organization in a narrow and self-serving way or through the prism of merging two companies and the ensuing integration of strategy, operations, and cultures. An example of leaders choosing the narrow self-serving route can be found when public relations tag lines are utilized to portray an image that is out of sync with the experience of the customer and/or employee. A company may chose to use the words globalization, or high tech or industry innovator, etc., when in fact they never deliver such a value proposition. Sound bite leadership produces at best skepticism in its customers and employees and in the worst-case scenario cynicism. The impact on the culture can be extremely harmful if the leadership fails to intervene immediately to correct. Corporations today are under increasing scrutiny and pressure to act in economically, environmentally, socially, and ethically responsible ways. Each of these areas must be visibly represented in the identity of today's global organization. Mergers and the ensuing integration activities provide an organization with an opportunity to shape the new emerging company's identity to meet today's rigorous expectations of both customers and employees.

Ackerman (2000) cites a Conference Board survey (1999) which, after interviewing a number of business leaders, reported three factors that were critical to ensuring success of the post-merger organization:

1. clear articulation (by leadership) and understanding (by employees) of the new company's basic identity, core values, and business strategy;
2. a strong underlying economic model of the organization; and
3. the philosophy and style of the CEO inspires confidence in the new entity's potential.

The power of identity was described in the Conference Board report as "the firm's identity supported by its core values and business strategy, helps to create a common understanding and commitment among all employees". Ackerman states:

The mechanics of integration are most dramatically evident today in globalization, which, in its own unique way, is prodding companies to wrestle with the notion of identity more seriously than ever before. Globalization is forcing a slow but steady integration of national markets and economies. Within far-flung organizations, it is driving the integration of experience, talent, beliefs, and passions among people who don't know each other, who come from different countries, and who don't speak the same language or share the same customs. Yet these people have been brought together to compete in territories where there is no end to the challenges they are being asked to meet. "Who are we?" has never been a more pressing question.

And yet, if we "Google" globalization we have millions and millions of links made available to us. The volume of information on globalization is so large that defining globalization and more importantly how it is being defined and acted upon in our business organizations is critical for all constituencies — business leaders, employees, customers, stakeholders, politicians, and citizens of the world. It is a 21st-century imperative that we gain a deeper understanding of: What is the globalization of business? Where did it come from? And which organizations have achieved a degree of success in globalizing their businesses?

Leadership, learning, and change are converging in the global business world to form business cultures that when they click are capable of producing enormous economic value to their customers, employees, stakeholders, and communities. When they lose their sense of identity their culture becomes fragmented and, in turn, destroys the value proposition of the organization. The challenge for all organizations — large or small — is for their leaders to understand what strategic learning and leading change means to them and to use the power of a sharply defined identity to create and recreate themselves through their employees as the meaning of globalization changes in an ever-changing world. Peter Drucker (1998) notes leadership/management is a social discipline that deals with "the behaviors of people and institutions ... the social universe has no natural laws as the physical sciences do. It is subject to continuous change. This means that assumptions that were valid yesterday can become invalid and, indeed, totally misleading in no time at all". Each of us must be vigilant to ensure that our organizations serve us in meeting the needs of people throughout the world.

Globalization and all it implies in the modern era for leadership, learning, and change is not a new phenomenon. The section that follows discusses the historical evolution of globalization of business enterprises and provides some examples of globalization in action.

What is Globalization

In the shadow of Wyoming's Grand Teton Mountains, a distinguished group of bankers and economists were leaving for the Federal Reserve's annual retreat. They spent the better part of three days in deep discussion grappling with the challenges surfacing from the defining force of our age — globalization. They listened and interacted with some of the world's leading academic economists who one after another, when pressed, sheepishly admitted the process and outcomes of globalization are not clearly understood — even after decades of study by some of the best minds in economics. Imagine attending a similar retreat dedicated to discussing and understanding globalization in relationship to industrialization, political policy, technology, information sharing, and social/cultural impact. Imagine coming away from the retreat with lots of new ideas and perspectives shared, but with very little progress in making meaning of what you heard and saw. Welcome to globalization in the 21st century. Such retreats and their outcomes and resultant feelings of excitement to be living at a time of enormous economic, social, and political change and fear that we will not be able to master the complexity of the current world give a human face to the millions of links that the "Google" search yielded.

Wikipedia, a click away from the "Google" search results, defines globalization as

The increasing interdependence, integration, and interaction among people and Corporations in disparate locations around the world. It is an umbrella term which refers to a complex of economic, trade, social, technological, cultural, and political interrelationships.

The term globalization, within a business context, is generally credited with the publishing of Theodore Levitt's (1983) Harvard Business Review article. Over 20 years later, there is still controversy over the Levitt article. Abdelal (2006) states

"Everyone says the article is wrong and everyone reads it 20 years later". Most agree that many of Levitt's futurist predictions were wrong. However, most agree that Levitt gave business managers a new way of looking at their markets and by provoking them with challenging questions changed the nature of the debate in the business community — then and now. Researchers and other interested observers and commentators such as Hohnen (2005), Robertson (2003), and Sheshabalaya (2006) have identified three waves or rounds of globalization. Large multinational corporations have dominated the shaping of the third wave/round starting after World War II. Prior to the focus on globalization of business enterprises there were two other distinct waves/rounds of globalization.

The First Wave/Round

The first wave takes us back to ancient times, well before the interchange of goods and services between different societies or civilizations. Ideas were the first medium of exchange across such civilizations as China, India, Greece, and Rome. Arabs are generally credited with transferring Indian science, medicine, and literature to the western world. As these civilizations developed the capability to produce goods and services, so did the trading between these vastly different cultures and societies. Hohnen (2005) notes "On the trade front, anthro-pological evidence suggests that humans have communicated and traded over vast distances for thousands of years. Marco Polo may have been the first Westerner to open a supply chain with China, but he didn't invent the concept". There was also a darker side to globalization during this wave. Tribal lords, religious leaders, and conquerors often plundered the local resources when needed to stimulate trading. Also cheap or free labor in the form of slaves was often employed to construct buildings, roadways, bridges, aqueducts, and so on. All this took place well before the creation of corporations to carry on the development and trading of goods and services.

The Second Wave/Round

The second wave/round of globalization started during the great colonial period that followed the maritime explorers such as Columbus, Diaz, and da Gama. It was during this period that European nation states created the Chartered Corporation. The Dutch and British East Indies Companies were set up to facilitate the active exchange/trading of goods and services as well as ideas across the known world. Perhaps the most powerful force for change in the second wave was industrialization in the production of goods and services. Also major changes in the transportation system, e.g. steamships followed by major improvements in communications systems such as wireless telegraphy. The formal financial flow of capital was also a major innovation during this wave through the banking systems and treasury concept.

Up until the 19th century there was an equality or equity between China, India, Europe, and America in reaping the benefits of global trade. As the 20th century approached, China's and India's position started to diminish and Europe and America's stared to sharply improve. The latter two have seen large-scale improvements to the health and well being of their citizenry including abundant food supplies, housing and medicines/hospitals, etc. The concepts of freedom, equality, and liberty also started to rise in Europe and America during this period which stimulated efforts of the citizenry to continue innovating ways to increase the trading of goods and services across ever-widening geographic circles. The 21st century is seeing the rapid rise of China's and India's position in the global economy as well as the improved position of Europe through the formation of the European Community and America's continued dominance innovating products and services. Questions are being raised as to whether these shifts in the global economy are sustainable. Will other players emerge to dominate the economy making it a more complex world to do business in?

The Third Wave/Round

The third wave/round continues today. Modern corporations, the descendants of the Dutch and British West Indies Companies, have formalized the way they develop their business strategy, their structure, operating processes, as well as the culture or environment they encourage, as they execute their strategy. This formalization, if followed, ensures a more orderly and smooth, as well as profitable, exchange of goods and services. Whether or not it enables or facilitates the organization's employees to learn, innovate, and change quickly as worldwide conditions change is very much a matter of debate. These corporations have and continue to amass enormous asset bases, in some cases, easily surpassing the economic value of entire countries.

The core customer base of these corporations is the growing middle class, well established in Europe and America, and rapidly growing in China and India. These middle class constituencies have increasingly well educated people who, through such mediums as the Internet and satellite/cable TV, are constantly searching for goods and services out of their geographic area. Borderless and automated finance has enabled a swift and relatively risk free way for millions of people throughout the world to purchase goods and services created in cultures thousands of miles away. This includes cultures that on the surface appear to have little or nothing in common. Modern delivery services such as DHL, FedEx, or UPS efficiently and at low cost complete the exchange between the buyer and seller. These new technologies and delivery services have also enabled relatively small businesses to successfully compete with large multinational corporations. In fact, many large corporations fear being disintermediated from their customers by small organizations that learn faster what is working and what is not working and based upon their learning rapidly change their business strategy, structure, operating processes and if needed their culture/environment. Knowing what to change and possessing the will to speedily do so in the face of risk of failure is quickly emerging as a 21st century required global business capability.

We have come a long way from the merchants who crossed the Arabian Desert to exchange their ideas with European nation states. There seems to be an unending, unquenchable appetite by consumers for the fruits of globalization whether it is innovative ideas, products, or services. A negative view of globalization postulates that the entire world's people will not benefit from the globalization of business enterprises. In the process of moving ideas, products/services, and people across the regions of the world, there will be winners and losers. We saw that in the first and second waves of globalization, the exploitation of resources as well as people in producing goods and services. Modern corporations have committed themselves to the global world of business and have been actively working on defining and operationalizing the global enterprise.

Defining the 21st-Century Business Enterprise

Strategy execution, and more importantly how to exceed stakeholder and financial analysts expectations, keeps CEO's around the world up at night. The more concisely the organization understands itself and the environment it operates in, as well as, how it develops its people to execute its strategy, the more likely it is to dominate its industry. Superior performance exhibited by more innovative products/services and the organizational prowess to deliver to their customers on time, quality, and at or below competitors cost is the defining capability of the 21st-century global corporation. Unfortunately, a clear concise definition of globalization has been eluding theorists as well as business leaders, which in turn impacts the clarity around the identity of the organization.

Globalization has been defined in a multitude of ways:

What do we mean when we say we live in an increasingly global world? ... If you are a CEO of Black & Decker, it means that, in reviewing your Strategy for the North America power tools market, you look at the strategies of competitors such as Makita and Bosch not only in North America but also worldwide. If you are the chairman of British Steel; it means you wake up every morning acutely aware of the fact that over 60 percent of your company's shares are owned by Americans rather than by perhaps more patient local investors ... And, last but not least, if you are a recent MBA and a junior manager at Procter & Gamble, you vow never to forget that you do not have a prayer of ever making it into the top ranks of the company unless you combine superb on-the-job performance with extensive international experience.

Govindarajan and Gupta (2000, p. 274)

A different perspective and definition:

Globalization is the integration of business activities across geographical and organizational boundaries. It is the freedom to conceive, design, buy, produce, distribute, and sell products and services in a manner which offers maximum benefit to the firm without regard to the consequences for the individual geographic location or organizational units ... The global firm stands ready to respond to changing market conditions and opportunities by choosing the alternatives which are thought to be the best in the long run ... The global firm is not constrained by national boundaries as it searches for ideas, talent, capital, and other resources required for its success. In short, the global firm perates with few, if any, self-imposed geographical or organizational constraints on where or how it conducts its business operations".

Ray Reilly, University of Michigan, and Brian Campbell, TriMas Corporation, quoted in Barnett (1992, p. 322)

In addition to the complexity of how the global organization thinks of its identity, there are also a number of paradox's to work through to be a successfully run global enterprise whether a for-profit business or not-for-profit or governmental agency. In leadership development programs, participants often express their difficulty with holding two opposing ideas in their thoughts and being able to think through an action plan to resolve the situation. Noel Tichy (University of Michigan, quoted in Barnett, 1992, p. 322) identified three such paradox's managers of global organizations must deal with:

1. global economies of scale and local customization,
2. transnational and domestic mind-sets, and
3. speed and quality.

Clearly a winner in the global marketplace demonstrates the ability of its leaders and employees to make sense of a complex environment and navigate successfully the paradoxes' noted above. They are facing these challenges each and every day in their functional areas as well as coordinating cross-functional responses. Some organizations are rapidly building their human capability in this area.

Globalization in Action

Not a week goes by without the business press and TV news showcasing a success or failure related to a global business. Historically, financial results were the primary measure used in reporting these stories. Now, while financial results are part of the story, there are also two additional elements that have captured our interest. These stories, in addition to how well they did in creating profits, now focus on environmental and social impact. Organizations that aspire to long-term success are paying serious attention to this triple bottom line — economic results, environmental and social impact on the communities in which they operate, and indeed to the world.

Globalization, overall, has and will continue to create enormous opportunities for individuals, companies, and countries. Over the last decade the global economy has withstood countless natural disasters, currency crises, wars and civil disturbances, erratic energy supplies and prices, and glacial progress in negotiating and implementing DOHA, the EU constitution. The US suffered the 9/11 terrorist attacks and the resulting uneasiness moved throughout the world that no one is safe anywhere or at anytime. And yet there was a stability and resilience found in the global economy. More and more companies of all sizes and locations have been globalizing themselves in spite of the negative forces.

Every company entering or expanding its presence in the global business arena asks itself the same question — do we have the right strategy and organization structure to capture and keep our share of the global economy? Before digging deeper into this area in Chapter 2, a few examples of some organizations that have gone global in spite of the negative forces discussed earlier are given.

IBM

IBM is often mentioned as one of the truly global corporations in the world even before its newest initiative on globalizing itself was released. IBM is working hard to become a model corporate citizen of the world with respect to delivering superior economic returns while respecting the environment and the societies/cultures in which it produces and delivers its products and services. As Sam Palmisano, Head of IBM, stated in a Financial Times Interview (Guerrera and Waters, 2006) "The globally integrated enterprise is a better way to organize business — with huge benefits for the developed and developing nations".

The essence of IBM's approach is to foster amongst their leadership a global management approach. Historically multinational corporations like IBM, Ford, and General Motors to name a few moved only production/manufacturing facilities offshore to reap the benefits of lower costs. Research and Development and other high-skill knowledge-based activities were kept in the home country — the US. IBM is now focusing on a radical transformation described in Business Week (Hamm, 2006). IBM has identified two major challenges to successfully building and sustaining their globally integrated company:

1. developing a skilled cadre of business leaders, who are capable of producing a continuous stream of product and service innovations; and
2. a diverse workforce that is engaged and passionate and can deliver these innovations at or above quality, at or below cost, and before the competition comes to market.

IBM is actively reorganizing around skill lines and not just geography. With a global workforce of over 200,000, this is no insignificant leadership challenge or change to the organization's identity. In addition, IBM is focusing on centrally coordinating, through its corporate function, operations worldwide to ensure more effective service delivery, lower prices to customers, and lower costs of operations. Truly embracing paradox and looking to win for all stakeholders is IBM's goal.

IBM has identified four critical elements to successfully executing its global business strategy:

1. Eliminating the Multinational strategy/structure — no longer running a mini-IBM in each country.
2. Performing work where it is most competitive to do so — India, China, Tulsa, etc.
3. The "A team" concept — new client engagements are staffed to suit customers needs with personnel selected from around the globe depending on skills needed/costs.
4. Staying out of commodity businesses where skills are not important and cost is the primary criteria.

The global integration initiative has also spurred employees to innovate, collaborate, and share learning by creating a volunteer global collaboration network. The purpose of the network is to support each other with projects. While IBM has taken a huge step in the strategic learning area it remains to be seen if the leadership can bring the changes through while improving IBM's revenue growth and cost savings. Strategic learning alone is not enough to convince investors to hold onto their stock. Leading successful change must be an integral part of strategic learning especially in global organizations where investors worldwide show little tolerance for delays in improving earnings.

GE

GE takes a different approach to the globalization of its business operations. They share the same goals of improving revenues while reducing costs throughout their value chain. The GE value chain is dependent on new technologies bringing improvements to the global supply chain they utilize to build innovative products and deliver them to their customer base. New high-technology approaches to supplying the materials to the manufacturing sites have the potential to add value to the customers by providing state-of-the-art equipment whether it is jet engines, microwave ovens, or medical diagnosis equipment. GE expects nearly half of its $163 billion in revenue this year to come from outside the US (Kranhold, 2006). The Financial Times (Guerrera, 2006) reports that within 3 years GE will make the majority of its products outside the US. GE see's its primary opportunity in taking cost advantage out of the manufacturing process through the Global Factory concept. The GE culture is well known from the Jack Welch approach and continuation by Jeffrey Immelt of demanding superior financial returns of its managers. Equally well known is the GE policy of weeding out its poor performers usually the bottom 10 percent.

Immelt is committed to leveraging learning and change prowess of his leadership team. He cites the example of the aircraft-engine division that made it through 9/11 because they knew their customers and their needs cold — "they had knowledge. They had gut feel. They had intuition". Immelt goes on to say "The businesses that work best here are businesses that had real deep roots in the industry they were in". There is not a substitute for a deep knowledge base of your customer's business strategy and how your strategy and operations supports them. Immelt is also committed to keeping managers in their assignment for longer time periods than has been the practice. Their learning's can be a competitive advantage if they are there to lead the changes necessary from natural or manmade disasters. Senior leadership has to balance this longer time in job with the manager's long-term career aspirations. Too long in a role may cause a negative feeling in the manager and their passion for the organization may suffer. Also a key component of the GE globalization strategy is increasing their manager's appetites for taking greater business risks without fearing the loss of their jobs. Taking increased risk is no easy task for these managers given GE's history under both Welch and Immelt of firing poor performers. This will require a major change to the GE culture to take hold and is necessary for all global companies to take increasingly greater risks.

IBM and GE are but two examples of the globalization of multinational corporations dedicated to facing the new world that globalization is presenting. Having a global vision is a prerequisite as the organization prepares to compete against known and more importantly unknown competitors who are determined to beat these old-line companies in the global marketplace. A world where strategy, structure, operations, and culture are no longer easily understood and communicated to employees and customers alike. This world insists on continuous innovation and flawless execution. Also critical to sustained success is the capability of the business leaders not only to execute current strategy but also to engage their employee's passion in taking on new challenges as they surface. Organizations that hold onto the past where leadership positions are awarded not on merit and ability, but on who knows who and political favor will not be able to compete. There are more questions than answers for business leaders who are building global organizations. The challenges that they face are discussed in Chapter 2.

References

Abdelal, R. "Historical Perspective: Leavitt Shaped the Debate." S. Silverthorne (ed.). HBS Working Knowledge, June 12, 2006.

Ackerman, L. D. *Identity is Destiny: Leadership and the Roots of Value Creation*. San Francisco, CA: Barrett-Koehler Publishers, 2000.

Barnett, C. K. "The Global Agenda for Research and Teaching in the 1990s." In V. Puck, N. M. Itchy, and C. K. Barnett (eds.). *Globalizing Management: Creating and Leading the Competitive Organization*, New York: Wiley, 1992.

Conference Board Survey. "Post Merger Integration Successes." July, 1999, cited in Ackerman (2000).

Drucker, P. *Fortune Magazine Interview*, 1998.

Govindarajan, V., and Gupta A. "Analysis of the Emerging Global Arena." *European Management Journal* 18(3) (2000), 274–284

Guerrera, F., and Waters, R. "IBM Chief wants End to Colonial Companies." *Financial Times*, June 12, 2006.

Hamm, S. "Big Blue Shift: IBM is Reorganizing Its Global Workforce to Lower Costs Without Skimping on Service." *Business Week*, under Information Technology/Globalization, June 5, 2006.

Hohnen, P. "The G8, Globalization, and the Last Wave." Originally published as The Ethical Corporation – June 30, 2005, available at www.globalpolicy.org, The Global Policy Forum, 2005.

Kranhold, K. "The Immelt Era: Five Years Old, Transforms GE." *Wall Street Journal*, September 11, 2006.

Levitt, T. "Globalization of Markets." *Harvard Business Review*, 1983.

Rhinesmith, S. H. *A Managers Guide to Globalization: Six Skills for Success in a Changing World*. New York: Irwin, 1996.

Robertson, R. *The Three Waves of Globalization: A History of a Developing Global Consciousness*. London & New York: Zed Book, 2003.

Sheshabalaya, A. "The Three Rounds of Globalization." Originally published in The Globalist, October 19, 2006, available at www.globalpolicy.org, The Global Policy Forum, 2006.

2

Challenges in Building Global Organizations

Globalization, as we saw in Chapter 1, often defies specific and permanent definition. Some organizations chose to exploit similarities across the geographies they operate in and they develop a strategy and structure that produces a standard product with little or no variation. Their product development, manufacturing and marketing strategies, and operations are coordinated centrally through a corporate or home office structure. Ulrich Lerner (Wiesmann, 2006), the CEO of Germany's Henkel, approachs global strategy for his company's products in one of three ways:

1. A global product with a global brand — this is a product that is usually the result of innovation and consumers not realizing they needed the product — for global companies these products provide the management with the opportunity to closely control continued product development, sales, and production from a central or home office location. MacDonald's 'Big Mac' and Apple's iPod are examples.
2. A global product with a local brand — these products usually come from acquisitions and can be carefully standardized over time to realize the economies of scale found in number 1. Personal grooming products such as the US brand Right Guard can be modified over time to meet the cultural demands of other regional markets.

3. A local product with a global brand — these products sell well in one country but do not do well in another country. These products are the most costly to maintain and further innovate on and rarely if ever can be modified cheaply enough to bring to true global status. Employees who aspire to global leadership positions most likely will not want to be associated with these products although well managed they can contribute significantly to a company's profits. A laundry detergent such as Persil in the Middle East has a unique set of product characteristics that fit the market there but cannot be easily or economically modified for sale in other parts of the world.

Other organizations select a more complicated approach to their strategy. According to Ghemawat (2003), these companies focus both on the similarities between countries as well as the differences. A company that is globalizing using a focus on similarities between countries is looking to extend its existing business model wherever it can and to make minor changes to the model to gain economies of scale. In contrast, a company that focuses on differences takes their companies leadership and employees down an entirely different path. Differences trigger a challenge to ones mind-set about how a business should operate in a country and across a variety of countries. This mind-set shift due to global strategy choices can lead the organization, its teams, and individuals to new and innovative approaches to product design, manufacturing, and marketing. Learning and the ensuing changes required for the organization to succeed can result in the transformation of the company and perhaps the industry. Designing an organization around difference or diversity adds complexity, ambiguity, and introduces dilemmas and paradoxes for managers to face and solve. When you try to draw an organization chart for a global company, you quite often stop after a very short time, after realizing it may not accurately reflect the way the organization gets its work done. Ward (2001) provides a key principle of designing global organizations — "design the organization to make it more effective, not to make it easier to manage". When leaders, managers, and employees practice strategic learning and lead the change needed, their organization can weather the uncertainties in strategy and structure inherent in global business. Ghemawat (2003) suggests that leaders who utilize both the strategy of similarities and differences can deliver outstanding financial results and create leaders who can master the paradoxes and complex issues that prevail in today's business environment. Jeffrey Immelt was CEO of GE Medical Systems (GEMS) from 1997 to 2000 prior to his becoming CEO of all GE. Immelt utilized both approaches to building a successful global strategy for GEMS by focusing on both the similarities and differences between his competitors and then developing an acquisition strategy to capitalize on these criteria. He also performed a similar analysis and execution plan for production capabilities and costs in different countries. When both innovative product design and cost efficient production come together, they produced enormous economies of scale as well as competitive advantage.

While no single strategy and structure works in the global business arena, Joyce et al. (2003) asked a straightforward question — What really works? They followed this core question up with the following: Why do a few companies thrive in the worst of times, contradicting all the misfortunes that afflict their competitors? Why do great companies stumble even during the best of times? The authors went on to conduct a systematic large-scale study of the practices that create business winners. They found eight management practices — four primaries and four secondary — that directly correlated with superior performance measured by total return to shareholders. The four primary practices:

1. devise a clearly stated focused strategy,
2. develop flawless operational excellence,

3. create a performance-oriented culture, and
4. build a fast, flexible, flat company structure.

The secondary practices were:

1. retain talented people and find more of them,
2. keep leadership committed to the business,
3. develop innovations that transform your industry, and
4. make growth happen with mergers and partnerships.

Their research went on to confirm that firms that excelled in the four primary and two of the secondary practices had a better than 90 percent chance of being winners. The authors believe that these are universal practices valid irrespective of the organization. They noted that books such as Gerstner' on transforming IBM or Welch on leading GE may or may not fit the challenges a leadership team faces in their own organization. Strategic learning is the capability that connects the above practices to enable all organizations to improve strategy execution. Strategic learning occurs when an individual, team, or organization experiences a change in perspective or understanding about the strategy or the resources and activities needed to successfully execute the strategy. Strategic learning may take place during the execution of the strategy or in a post-strategy execution review. Reflection either during strategy execution efforts or after is a critical process for all involved to undertake. Reflection coupled with dialogue between involved parties can yield clear lessons learned and lead to identifying needed changes in the strategy, structure, and/or resources. Strategic outsourcing provides a situation where we can see the four primary practices as well as the strategic learning capability of an organization. We will also see the need to globalize HR to support today's global business enterprises. APC, a European-based Pharma company, which is discussed in greater detail in Part II, decided to change its strategic direction and outsource some of its clinical trials.

A Case at Hand

Every week, it seems, the popular business press showcases organizations across industries and geographies outsourcing yet another part of their operations. The first operations to be outsourced were not core competencies such as payroll, security, food services, and copy/mail/call centers. A number of organizations are now moving to outsource core operations or competencies. In a recent special report on outsourcing in *Business Week*, Engardio and Enhorn (March 21, 2005) ask, "First came manufacturing. Now companies are farming out R&D to cut costs and get new products to market faster: Are they going too far?" According to the authors of the *Business Week* article, Motorola, Royal Philips Electronics, Palm One, and Samsung are some of the companies that outsource core parts of their operations. Although these companies are well-known household brands, the firms that actually do the outsourced work are virtually unknown. Several large pharmaceutical companies (Pharmas) outsource not just routine commodity-like operations but parts of their internal value chain, which are considered core competencies of the organization. According to the *Business Week* article, "CEOs are rethinking their R&D operations, wondering where mission critical research ends and commodity work begins". According to senior managers within the pharmaceutical industry, however, these instances are not seen as outsourcing of commodities but instead viewed as strategic partnering with third party providers who can complete these tasks faster, cheaper, and at a higher quality than internally.

A Business Case for Strategic Outsourcing

Pharmas are feeling the need to significantly improve performance across the entire value chain: from early molecule identification to commercializing the drug. The cost of bringing a drug from discovery to market can take 12 plus years and approximately 1 billion dollars in investment. Pricing pressures are now being felt in an industry where price was never an issue and where profit margins were the envy of many CEO's in other industries. Governmental organizations, hospital chains, pharmacy benefit managers, among others, are all asking for reduced pricing due to their volume purchasing capability. Pharmas are also being asked to look beyond blockbuster drugs to serving smaller patient populations that have unmet medical needs. Developing countries are asking for assistance in meeting drug needs at substantially reduced prices.

These issues, along with globalization, are pressuring the pharmaceutical industry to be both a product innovator as well as a low-cost producer. Having people who can adjust to a culture of "innovator" and "low-cost producer" at the same time is key to the success of such a strategy. This is a challenge in the best of times. In an environment where the industry dynamics and career opportunities are in constant flux, recruiting, acculturating, developing, rewarding, and retaining highly educated talent require a high degree of sensitivity and skill. These human resource practices can also provide the needed competitive advantage if the leadership of the organization develops these skills. This is particularly true of knowledge-intensive industries. Strategic outsourcing of core competencies can provide significant business advantage to such an organization, but it can also cause massive disruption to strategy execution. Making a business case for strategic outsourcing and communicating and implementing this strategy needs to be done with much care.

Typically, in a pharmaceutical company, building a business case for strategic outsourcing requires measuring the value of the outsourcing arrangement. A cross-functional team is assembled and charged with coming up with a comprehensive business case to present to senior management. This team must involve finance, legal, human resources, marketing, and research to determine key criteria for the case.

Certain financial (such as cost savings, return on assets, or return on capital employed) and non-financial measures (such as deliverables on time, at quality and on cost, innovation and intellectual property, and opportunities created) are standard in the industry. However, managers with experience in strategic outsourcing are aware of a number of pitfalls in this process and include other criteria such as monitoring the quality of the working relationship between the two teams and the investment in time and energy needed to have two teams from different organizational cultures, performance-management/rewards systems, and leadership. The business case includes ways of anticipating problems such as mistrust in relationships, handling of persistent problems, level and satisfaction of communication between the teams from the company and the outsourcing firm, and clarity in identifying responsibility centers.

The business case must also include organizational issues. Successful cases have the following characteristics: highly collaborative working relationships where mutual trust is evident, with minimal need for enforcement through the legal contract. Collaboration is defined in terms of the teams' ability to adhere to specific, mutually agreed to ground rules regarding keys issues such as communication, control of team meetings and project assets, data collection and analysis, and decision-making. The business case must include how and when unanticipated situations are to be handled. Guidelines should be provided for teams to "escalate" an issue to the next level in their respective organizations.

Legal issues, including potential for conflicts of interest, are clearly laid out in the business case. Several potential outsourcing providers are identified and a comparative analysis is done. This phase is often very long, protracted, and frustrating. Internal project champions for this outsourcing decision are a critical factor in its success.

At this stage, discussions and negotiations with the outsourcing firm move into the actual contracting stage. There are usually numerous discussions and rewriting of the contracts before both parties begin discussing the substantive goals of the outsourcing project. Next, begins a "project management" phase, which details the expected deliverables, roles/accountabilities, timelines, and budget responsibilities. Both parties often appoint specific personnel to handle the project.

Executing the Strategic Outsourcing Decision

The Executive Committee (EC) of the firm may evaluate the business case and recommend proceeding after all stakeholders have been briefed and their questions and concerns answered. In this phase questions around financial, legal, quality, security, timeliness, and impact on the overall strategy execution and competitive positioning of the organization are addressed. In large complex organizations, this phase can take up to a year or longer to wind through all the pathways and to satisfy internal and external stakeholders.

Vendor selection is often done in parallel to this phase if the executives leading the outsourcing initiative are confident that internal and external stakeholders will bless the project. Vendors that most closely follow the existing internal processes to minimize the internal team's learning curve are sought. The reputation of the vendor for building strong relationships with internal team personnel is also a crucial element in the selection. Relationship problems are expensive and highly time consuming to resolve. Poor or adversarial relationships impact quality, speed, and drain the benefits that the outsourcing organization is trying to achieve. Collaboration, joint problem-solving and decision-making are critical elements of an effective outsourcing arrangement. These are hard to achieve across different organizations whose own employees share an internal culture, values, performance/ rewards, and development processes unique to their respective organization. As a result, companies considering outsourcing may develop vendor company profiles that specify the level of product and technology capability as well as the vendor's track record of performing across the entire outsourcing value chain. There are consulting organizations that provide this service. They conduct contract negotiations as well, and build the internal team and infrastructure — including IT support — needed to make the outsourcing arrangement operational.

APC Outsources Clinical Trials

APC R&D decided to outsource some of its core operations across some therapeutic areas. They went through a number of issues and processes discussed above. APC was formed through a merger of two large pharmaceutical companies A and P. During the post-merger integration phase, the senior team was careful to involve both internal and external stakeholders in formulating and implementing strategy. This included their decision to scale up their involvement in strategic outsourcing. Significant differences of opinion surfaced. Champions of outsourcing discovered that they had to play the roles of diplomats as well as technical gurus. The most compelling part of the business case focused on freeing up the brainpower and on the ability to drive innovation across the research and development value chain, as opposed to managing clinical trials. The business case is bolstered by showing increase in the speed of completing the trials at quality, reliability, ethical standards, and at low cost.

As background, "A" had already been involved in outsourcing clinical trials. Each therapeutic area handled its own outsourcing. "A" had outsourced approximately 40% of their clinical trials prior to merger. "P" had never engaged in outsourcing anything in the R&D area. "P" had outsourced some of its sales activities. APC was facing a very enviable situation. A rich pipeline across all the phases of research and development was pressuring the organization to speed up its commercialization cycle. Both internal and external stakeholders were confident in their proposed change in strategic direction because of "A's" expertise in the area. More innovative products delivered to patients in a shorter time period would put APC ahead of its competition economically.

As APC gained more and more experience in strategic outsourcing, it also recognized the need to invest in more internal resources dedicated to coordinating outsourcing. As a result, APC ran the following advertisement for a manager:

MANAGER, STRATEGIC OUTSOURCING MANAGEMENT

APC, a world leader in developing Pharmaceuticals in a number of therapeutic areas, is committed to expanding its leadership position. Embrace this opportunity to join a group of diverse and talented individuals championed to take on innovation and change in our rapidly expanding organization. Manage all aspects of strategic outsourcing including vendor management, financial management, and contract development/negotiation for clinical trials ... role requires the ability and foresight to proactively identify operational and/or relationship issues and to resolve issues in a timely manner so that time, cost, and/or quality targets are achieved ... No direct oversight of other employees. Indirectly the role is responsible for other employees in various capacities ... [on] cross-functional team members.

No one involved in strategic outsourcing would deny the need for such a manager. However, was this enough? APC's experience in outsourcing clinical trials has been mixed. There have been some resounding successes and some very visible failures. The salient issues have been problems in leadership, not in structuring or design. It appears as though a different kind of leadership is needed to implement strategic outsourcing decisions. One senior business leader of APC said:

It's not about project management — it's about leadership, team leadership; global teams cross at least two different organizations and god knows how many cultures and time zones. You can't bet the farm [core competence] and have anything less than your best leaders stepping up and delivering on the promise. That's the organizational challenge we have ahead.

At APC no one interviewed could explain the "strategic outsourcing manager" position advertised and how it fit into the organization's overarching strategy. The position description just appeared one day without context or explanation. A number of questions came to mind regarding APC's strategic intent around this outsourcing position. There were serious questions concerning the impact of this job specification on the very culture and values of the organization. Was this a pilot to gain experience in the area or a commitment to strategic outsourcing as part of its core strategy to gain an innovation edge on its competition? In either scenario, APC could have followed some very basic principles in working with their employees to understand the senior leadership's thinking about and level of commitment to strategic outsourcing. Outsourcing of any type has a profound impact on an organization's culture and, so it did with APC.

At APC, the job posting for the strategic outsourcing position caused a wave of curiosity followed by a wave of uncertainty and fear. There had been no communication from senior management about their intent concerning strategic outsourcing. It seemed clear that an external candidate would fill the position. There was uncertainty about how strategic outsourcing would impact the performance management, talent management, and leadership development processes.

The rumor mill went immediately to work in the worst possible way. In the absence of facts, rumor had it that major portions of the internal value chain, as well as existing jobs and future jobs were being outsourced. People indicated unease about their ability to deliver on their current goals — especially those at the interfaces of the areas mentioned in the job announcement. Failure to deliver at high performance levels would preclude consideration in talent management for leadership development reserved for high potential individuals. Employees understood the systemic connection among performance management, talent management, and leadership development and the impact of this on their careers. They expressed concern that senior leadership did not seem to understand these connections.

APC and Strategic Learning

Announcement of strategic outsourcing can create fear in an organization. This fear is palpable in the employee ranks since no one feels safe in their jobs. Service levels are often improved by outside vendors, and management can reduce overhead processing costs in the short term. Outsourcing can negate years of effort that an organization spends in building a strong sense of community among its employees. This, in turn, can make retention difficult. Companies where senior leadership can create and sustain a feeling of community are highly admired. Strategic outsourcing tests the leadership of even such companies. The deeper a leader understands the connections between culture and the organization's strategy and their people, the more effectively they can compete in today's competitive marketplace. Preserving a sense of community is critical to mitigating the adverse effects of strategic outsourcing.

It is widely acknowledged that culture, while easy to discuss, is very difficult to change in any meaningful way. Outsourcing done poorly can trigger very serious problems in an organization's culture. The feeling of connectedness and belonging, so important to community and high performance, can very rapidly disappear if employees sense that their area of core competence is to be outsourced. Strategic outsourcing can seriously destabilize an organization; a challenge, that most leadership teams are ill equipped to handle.

Alternatively, strategic outsourcing offers the leadership teams the opportunity of strengthening employee commitment at the individual, team, and organizational level. Employees will look for strong and clear signs from senior leadership. Is the proposed strategic outsourcing a pilot or a major shift in strategy for the organization? Senior management can use a number of different media to communicate its intentions in this area. A President's page on the company intranet, town hall meetings with all employees, briefings for managers to communicate key strategic outsourcing messages to their people are different ways in which this can be achieved. Sufficient detail should be provided for employees to understand how strategic outsourcing fits into the strategy, mission, vision, and values of the organization.

Communication, while critical, is not sufficient to maintain employees' trust in the culture and leadership of the organization. Employees must also be able to see how the proposed strategic outsourcing will impact their current and future positions. Senior leadership should be able to explain in some detail, anticipated changes to the organization's structure, performance management, rewards, talent management, and leadership development philosophies and processes. These changes need to be thought out by senior management before announcing a strategic outsourcing initiative in the organization. All of the above areas must be well defined and openly communicated to secure employee support. This requires trust in senior management, which is a leadership quality that needs to be developed.

Similar to alliances or joint ventures, problematic issues surfaced very quickly after the contract for outsourcing was signed by APC. The taking of swift and direct action by both teams was critical to fixing the project and getting it back on track. Projects that proceeded smoothly were most often attributed to interpersonal chemistry and not to the skill of the team leaders. Projects were frequently terminated if relationship issues could not be quickly resolved. It was crucial that both teams assumed the responsibility to ensure open communication and to preserve management processes, such as the monitoring of team progress that would propel the project forward.

A subtler trend emerged concerning the skills of project leaders: few had been trained to lead or to participate in a strategic outsourcing project. As a rule, they were very experienced project managers but they lacked the confidence to successfully lead a strategic outsourcing team. They expressed the necessity for a skill set that was most likely different from the ones they possessed but could not articulate what that skill set might look like. Most indicated that they did strategic outsourcing part time in addition to their "real job".

Leading Strategic Outsourcing

What, when, and how to communicate are age-old questions with no easy answers. It gets much easier if the senior team has decided where and how strategic outsourcing fits into the company's strategic plan. This is particularly important since it is clear that strategic outsourcing will require substantial changes to the organization's reporting structure.

Strategic outsourcing should be positioned in the organization to attract the best and brightest an organization has to offer. When a strategic outsourcing manager reports to the CEO, it is sure to attract the best candidates internally as well as externally. Word goes out quickly into the industry environment how much an organization values the function's contribution to its strategy execution efforts. A direct report to the CEO conveys the importance to the organization and is best equipped to deal with the strategic implementation necessary.

The strategic outsourcing manager position can also be placed within support functions. Senior management must always remember that they are outsourcing parts of their core competence, not a commodity service or process. A very different perception about the significance of strategic outsourcing is evident if the reporting relationship is not at the CEO level but within each specific functional area. There is much less scope and potential impact on the strategy and its execution.

A well-designed and implemented performance-management process is also needed to ensure that strategic outsourcing will be understood by employees and implemented as effectively as possible. Seven performance differentiators may be identified:

- clarity of executives about their role in strategic outsourcing implementation;
- clarity of managers about their roles and responsibilities in strategic outsourcing;
- clarity of purpose and goals of strategic outsourcing in terms of the overall business strategy;
- performance measurement aligned to strategy;
- accountability of executives individually and as a team for outsourcing decisions; and
- ability of senior leadership to improve teamwork, collaboration, and culture and making this their top priority.

All of the above differentiators need to be embedded in a well-designed and implemented performance-management process. It was clear from APC's job description for their strategic outsourcing manager that the firm was unclear as to how the position fit into the overall strategy of a firm. And yet, it expected the manager to set goals around quality, time, and costs of the outsourced part of the internal value chain without much effort. However, the strategic outsourcing process is much more complex. There are interfaces, such as trial design and post-trial regulatory approval that need to be addressed. The strategic outsourcing process is not linear. There need to be discussions and modifications along the way. It is difficult to write specific service-level agreements with quantifiable outcome measures. In strategic outsourcing it may even be difficult to identify all the players. It would seem nearly impossible for APC's manager of strategic outsourcing to orchestrate this without face-to-face meetings with all of the work groups as well as with the provider's work team.

APC had a well-designed and developed strategic alliance/joint venture framework that could assist the organization in successfully implementing strategic outsourcing. The work groups from both companies in the alliance met frequently to discuss strategy, goals, measures, roles, etc., before the alliance was activated. Both sides had to feel equally prepared to execute the strategy to which they agreed. Team meetings took place virtually with an occasional face-to-face meeting needed to resolve issues. A person from each team involved in the goal and deliverable was designated to be the problem-solving liaison to the alliance and could initiate discussion around changes in strategy, goals, measures, roles, and deliverables. The EC gave the team wide latitude in making decisions as needed with only one reservation. Legal issues would have to be vetted by the legal counsel before the decision could be taken. Scheduled into the alliance were face-to-face debriefing sessions where the teams involved were encouraged to present their experience of the alliance to date in the form of a story. A facilitator and a graphic artist who rendered the stories in pictures as they were being told categorized the stories. Team participants allowed no formal presentations. The story's lessons learned were captured, and changes to the alliance strategy and processes were formalized in a report and sent to the senior executives for approval. Senior executives were encouraged to attend the story telling debriefings rather than reading about it in a standard power point presentation.

Strategic outsourcing is a form of strategic change. It needs to be implemented in the same manner. The organization's policies and systems of strategy implementation should be applied to the implementation of strategic outsourcing. Implementing such outsourcing as just an operational decision can be fraught with risks. Strategic outsourcing needs to be incorporated into an organization's talent management and leadership development processes or programs.

Conclusions

Outsourcing is stressful for employees and more so when an organization is globalizing. Strategic outsourcing is even more stressful. Organizational cultures are fragile ecosystems that are easily damaged and difficult to repair. Trust and sense of community, when shattered, can have significant impact on an organization's ability to execute its strategy and to attract and retain the best talent.

In a recent *Wall Street Journal* article Prahalad (June 8, 2005) stated:

> *The current outsourcing phenomenon is the start of a new pattern of innovation in the way we manage. The ability to fragment complex management processes and reintegrate them into the whole is a new capability ... the time to learn to manage with a global system of knowledge, products, services, and component vendors is now.*

Employees at APC expected their senior leaders to lead the way in the strategic outsourcing area. APC had invested heavily in developing their business leaders through formal executive educational experiences and challenging job assignments. Yet, most business leaders felt they were forced to take a reactive approach instead of a more productively proactive one. The convergence of various factors in APC's outsourcing process — APC's uneven communication of the leadership's intent behind strategic outsourcing, the organizational structure used to support strategic outsourcing, the search for external candidates to fill the new strategic outsourcing manager's role — created an environment of uncertainty for the employees regarding the current and potential status of their career at APC. Fortunately, the investment APC had made in developing their business leaders allowed these leaders to quickly identify and address the concerns of their employees.

Summarizing some of the lessons from APC's implementation of its outsourcing strategy, we see that to be successful: Senior leaders must articulate strategic direction before the outsourcing strategy is implemented. Where the strategic outsourcing function reports into and how it will be staffed are critical bits of information.

- Leadership must be capable of working with employees in the performance-management arena, including interdependent goal setting between employee and vendor, as well as creating rewards for successfully delivering the outsourcing project's goals. Coaching employees in conflict resolution as well as in leading a team where direct reporting relationships are non-existent must be part of every senior leader's toolkit.
- HR must take a leadership role in the talent management area by coaching line leaders who are responsible for strategic outsourcing implementation, by modifying talent management definitions, process, and communications. In addition, HR can play a major role in redefining the philosophy and guidelines found in the talent management materials that are available to employees.
- Leadership development must be redesigned to reflect the strategic outsourcing reality. Case studies, simulations, scenarios, etc., should be part of the supervisory, management, and leadership curriculums. Preparing line leaders to manage complex and ambiguous situations that arise from strategic outsourcing implementations, as well as to lead teams composed of people from two different organizations.
- A culture must be created that supports people, as strategic outsourcing becomes more and more prevalent in the strategic plan. There will be an impact on employee's current positions and rewards and on their continuing development and career growth in the organization. A critical component of this culture is a feeling of community amongst its employees. This leads to more open communications between the leadership and employees as well as the sharing of strategic learnings.

- Globalizing the strategic outsourcing function as well as the HR function provides the platform for articulating a coherent people strategy that fully supports the business strategy. A global head of strategic outsourcing would most likely report to the CEO. This sets the stage for properly resourcing the strategic outsourcing function from a business perspective. Strategic outsourcing is complex as well as risky from a business intelligence perspective. Implementing strategic outsourcing needs careful thought and visible leadership that is not seen in many organizations.

APC was committed to building a high-performing global team-based organization. HR would be critical to its success, Part II discusses how APC approached building a global team-based organization that its leadership believed was needed to create a new kind of Pharma Company. Part III expands on the globalization of HR and how with globalization, the role of HR must be reinvented.

Note: A Case at Hand is based on an article published by John (2006).

References

Engardio, P., and Einhorn, B. "Outsourcing Innovation." *Business Week*, March 21, 2005.

Ghemawat, P. "Globalization: The Strategy of Differences." Harvard Business School Working Knowledge for Business Leaders, November 10, 2003.

John, S. "Leadership and Strategic Change in Outsourcing Core Competencies: Lessons from the Pharmaceutical Industry." Human Systems Mgt 135–143, Amsterdam, Netherlands: IOS Press, 2006.

Joyce, W., et al. *What (Really) Works: The 4+2 Formula for Sustained Business Success*. Harper Collins: New York, 2003.

Prahalad, C. K. "The Art of Outsourcing." *Wall Street Journal*, June 8, 2005.

Ward, K. "Designing Global Organizations." In P. Kirkbride and K. Ward (eds.). *Globalization: The Internal Dynamic*. West Sussex, England: Wiley, 2001.

Wiesmann, G. "Brands that Stop at the Border." *Financial Times*, Business Life-Consumer Marketing, June 10, 2006.

3

Strategic Learning and Leading Change

The test of a good story isn't its responsibility to the facts as much as its ability to provide a satisfying explanation of events.

Philip Rosenzweig (2006)

Harold, Head of Global Marketing, refused to believe what had just happened. He had been struggling for over a year trying to get Global Marketing to really be global. The reception was over and he was on his way back to the office. Another long night answering e-mails, voicemails, and trying to convince himself he was not addicted to his blackberry, pager, and two cell phones. Harold like several other executives before him had just entered the world of strategic learning and leading change. He had not planned on it but it happened none the less. He had eagerly volunteered to come to speak at the first APC Executive development session. He knew his topic cold — The Global Matrix. Better yet he was asked to speak without slides. Make it conversational but with impact. He was in his element. After all he had been promoted to one of the most visible global roles in the newest pharma company and word on the street had it as the most promising. He had not admitted it publicly until tonight that this challenge was the most difficult he had ever faced. Failure was a distinct possibility and also not tolerated very well at APC. This was keeping him up at night — every night.

What happened at the Executive development session? Prior to his arrival, the participants had been asked to prepare a case study solution. The case study focused on APC's Global Matrix strategy and, more importantly, what was blocking strategy execution efforts. There were five teams of eight participants. Each team had representation from the business functions as well as major country/regions. After Harold spoke, the teams presented their solutions to him. They engaged him in a dialogue about the strengths and weaknesses of his strategy and execution efforts. They pressed him to lead the changes needed over the coming year to make global marketing a success story within APC.

The teams had identified three primary issues:

1. The global strategy required global teams. 9/11 had put a major scare into the organization regarding travel and so teams were encouraged to do 50 percent or more of their work virtually. Time zone differences, distance, multiple nationalities and cultures, and often the changing of team members due to conflicting country priorities added to the complexity of getting the strategy executed.
2. Lots of planning (face-to-face and remotely) and lots of activity were required. Little or no reflecting on the work process and results and what might need changing was currently practiced. One team mentioned the Deming (Plan, Do, Check, Act) Wheel. The check or reflection part of the process was not part of their processes.
3. Recognition from the management for team successes and feedback on failures was necessary. Currently, they had no way of knowing what management was thinking about their execution efforts.

The discussion also focused on the still heavily siloed country organizations. They were protecting their "turf" and they told Harold "the countries were winning".

Harold hedged on agreeing to specific changes, but promised them a speedy response. The response would come through Global HR (GHR) who had the primary responsibility for executive development as well as performance rewards, and talent management across the entire organization.

Harold, as host of the evening reception, charmed everyone present. Although after he left, many participants expressed concern that he would not commit to any change. Where was his sense of urgency? APC needed a global marketing success to convince or demonstrate to the world that the Pharma industry must transform itself to a global team-based strategy and leave the countries to sell the products.

On Monday, Harold sent an e-mail to GHR to distribute to the participants of last week's session. He committed to building more effective global teams by improving the dialogue and to share his learning's with the EC. He promised to champion the changes that surfaced from the global marketing teams directly to the EC (all global function heads and the CEO). Their voices would be heard and needed changes would be supported by an EC member.

GHR had orchestrated a major breakthrough in strategy execution.

Strategic Learning and Leading Change Hits the Fashion Industry

APC was leading the way in transforming the pharmaceutical industry. Its strategy, structure, operating processes, and culture were all in flux and causing lots of suffering and pain for all levels of the organization: senior leadership, management, and employees. Financial analysts, shareholders, and other stakeholders had little patience for organizations who did not immediately grasp the nature of the new business environment, devise clever ways to solve these problems and then rapidly change their organization as it braced itself for the cycle to repeat itself over and over again. It does not matter if you are in the auto business, energy, financial services, high tech, telecommunications, or fashion.

The leadership and employees in all these industries have to think and act in new/innovative ways about their strategy, structure, and culture. When changes are identified, it is expected that the leadership and employees of the organization will quickly implement the needed change. Failure to learn and/or change can result in a company losing its industry position and status. Those who can master this new paradigm can dominate their industry over decades. LVMH is such a story.

The LVMH Story

We will know 20 years from now what fashion is in Paris. Right now, there is general confusion.

Karl Lagerfeld (cited in Agins, p. 17, 1999)

Agins (1999) states: "The time when 'fashion' was defined by French designers whose clothes could be afforded only by the elite has ended. Now designers take their cues from mainstream consumers and creativity is channeled more into mass-marketing clothes than into designing them". By the late 1990s it was clear that the fashion industry had undergone radical change. There was a shift from actual clothing design capability to marketing expertise. Talented people would be drawn to the fashion industry, who a decade before would have never considered it a business career choice.

Bernard Arnault understood the paradigm shift in the early 1980s. He started building LVMH in 1984 by acquiring Christian Dior. He continued on an acquisition spree that focused entirely on luxury brand companies — "my relationship to luxury goods is really very rational. It is the only area in which to make luxury products". Arnault used a straightforward recipe — identify high-profile designers who created a lot of press and then use global marketing to sell the brand and its offerings to as many customers as possible — "The reason to be a designer is to sell". LVMH is now a multibillion dollar luxury brand organization whose primary capability is global marketing. Arnault, like Harold, was committed to strategic learning and then leading the necessary change to transform and dominate their respective industries.

A Deeper Look at Strategic Learning and Leading Change

A major paradigm shift had occurred, for Harold and Arnault, over a very short period of time. In less than a decade (short in comparison to a professional's career span of approximately 35–40 years) people entering their business field, as well as seasoned professionals, were facing an environment filled with ambiguity, parody, and complexity. This created true culture shock for the individual and the organization. Historical ways of doing things in an organization would no longer work.

Today's organizations are searching for people who can create innovative product design as well as brilliance in marketing to a mass audience. For many, this convergence of design and marketing expertise is best seen in the iPod. The iPod dominates its industry space. Some of the largest, best-resourced organizations have tried to unseat it, e.g. Hewlett Packard tried unsuccessfully. Despite there being nothing wrong with the HP strategy and product. The iPod has taken on cult-like status in the marketplace.

Strategic Learning Defined

Examples of strategic learning are all around us. We saw the success companies like IBM and GE are having in their respective marketplaces. Many old-line companies are also looking at their strategies and determining how effective they are at translating their strategy into competitive advantage. Every organization large or small, global or local, high tech or low faces unprecedented competition. Organizations no one has ever heard of before are becoming dominant forces in their industry space. They target other organizations' customers and lure them away by offering innovative products or services at lower costs. Large companies develop intricate competency models and complicated team initiatives that promise employees who adopt them that they will be working for an organization that is an industry leader. Everyone is shocked when a much smaller competitor successfully moves in on their customer base. These smaller companies, as well as some select large organizations, have perfected how to learn on the fly and then recreate themselves as necessary. They never rest on their laurels. They change everything if needed — strategy, operations, research, and culture when they internalize and reflect on lessons learned from their current performance. They do not stop at current performance. They look to the future using simulations and scenario planning. Their cultures support risk taking and the inevitable failures. Learning's are analyzed, internalized, and used to lead change.

Peter Engardio (2006) reported in Business Week "Multinationals from China, India, Brazil, and even Egypt are coming on strong. They're hungry — and want your customers. They're changing the global game". The Boston Consulting Group (BCG), reported in the same article, collecting data from 3,000 companies in 12 developing nations. They went on to identify 100 emerging multinationals that appear positioned to "radically transform industries and markets around the world". These companies have been able to identify the key knowledge and skills needed to innovate and execute at world class levels in a much shorter time cycle than others, including well-established competitors. Open access to capital, information, and talent levels are evolving as competitive advantage where in the past deep experience was "the" competitive advantage. Ram Charan cited in the Engardio article credits these high-potential emerging companies "... Their leaders are good executors who see niches in the global economy and can top world intellectual capital and financial markets to consolidate control across their industries". Social Network Analysis (SNA) talks of connectors — people who operate just as Charan indicates above. They are lifelong strategic learners who can fix present problems and create the future of their organization — sometimes simultaneously!

Guiding Principles of Strategic Learning

As discussed in Chapter 2, successful strategy execution is directly connected to an individual's, team and/or the organization itself to undergo a change in perspective or understanding of their strategy execution efforts. These insights can be the result of a formal review of execution efforts by leadership and management or external events that require a change in thinking about the strategy itself. Reflection and the ensuing dialogue on what is been learned and what must be changed can be invaluable to reformulate the strategy for communication throughout the organization. The speed with which an organization can accomplish this is often the deciding factor for which organization dominates their industry. Individual, teams, and their organizations can benefit from strategic learning by applying the following eight principles as they execute their current or reformulated strategy.

There are eight principles of strategic learning that have evolved from working with professional and financial service organizations and pharma/biotech companies. In addition to work experience, learning theorists such as Mezirow (1991), Watkins and Marsick (1993), and Schon (1987) have provided conceptual frameworks for making sense of these work experiences. In addition, coaching of the leadership of these organizations is provided to articulate and implement needed changes to their strategy, structure, operating processes, and/or culture. The first three principles focus on the individual and the following five on the organization.

1. Learning starts with the individual being open to learning from experience and from others in and outside of the organization.

2. Learning requires regular reflection on experience and other perspectives.
3. Learning leads to action, then reflection, and then testing the new learning with others.

Individual Learning becomes organizational strategic learning when:

1. Learning is directly connected/linked to strategy, vision, and values of the organization.
2. Learning leads to problem solutions as well as a source of innovation.
3. Learning is recognized and rewarded by the organization at the individual and team level.
4. Learning from failure is supported by the culture of the organization and is not punished.
5. Learning must be shared/transferred to other individuals, teams, and the larger organization, e.g. across functions, geographies, alliances, and strategic outsourcing partners.

The organizational commitment needed to institutionalize strategic learning is clear. Senior leadership must be role models of using strategic learning as a core process to solve problems and for innovation. At times, depending upon the business climate and competitive challenges discussed above it is an organization's culture that facilitates or impedes strategic learning and as we will see leads change as well. At other times, it is strategic learning that can create an opening for needed culture change to be acknowledged and acted upon if senior leadership has the courage to do so. Learning cultures provide an environment where all employees can explore alternative ways of doing things, experiment and risk failure whether solving a current business problem or innovating for the future, i.e. anticipating consumer needs and developing new products to satisfy those needs.

Cultural cues should clearly show that strategic learning is valued by the organization and in fact is one of the organization's values — to be lived everyday by all employees. This kind of cultural environment encourages people's minds and more importantly engages their spirit and passions as they perform their work. This kind of environment moves people to a place where obstacles in problem solving are seen as opportunities and where the future becomes a possibility. These cues can be clearly seen in organizations that focus their senior leadership and managers efforts in coaching their top talent. This coaching takes place in two primary areas. The first in coaching their top talent for high performance and second coaching for accelerated development. Strategic learning forms the foundation for these teachable moments between management and top talent in the organization.

Top talents reporting to leaders who excel at building organizational talent are more engaged, substantially less likely to leave and outperform their peers by up to 27%.

Corporate Executive Board (2006)

Performance and Development Coaching and Strategic Learning

A primary responsibility of management is to provide a culture that supports superior performance as well as provides exciting development opportunities for its top talent. By identifying and supporting those individuals who add the most value to their organization's strategy execution, an environment is created where highly talented people can flourish in their current role as they prepare to take on ever increasingly higher levels of responsibility. The shared commitment and passion between senior leadership and top talent is critical to an organization achieving its vision. Nurturing its top talent is a continuous process that starts within the performance management cycle with rigorous stretch goal setting that is supported by ongoing coaching to ensure high performance in their current role. The process continues by jointly discussing and each person owning their respective part of the accelerated development process. Together a manager and employee create a strategy for performance and continuous learning/development that as a senior APC leader said,

> *The challenge ... is to deliver new value today while simultaneously preparing for tomorrow. We need to get even better at what we do now, while at the same time, build the capabilities we'll require to be successful in the months and years to come. This is how, working together, we can all support our strategy and invent our future ...*

High-performance cultures share a similar philosophy for managing their top talent. They have the following guiding principles:

1. it is a core business process, not an event, woven into the fabric of the culture to ensure the development and continuity of leadership for the organization;
2. driven by the organization's business strategy and senior management involvement;
3. identifies talent early in their careers and accelerates their development;
4. develops all employees but invest heavily in top talent; and
5. rewards strategic learning and change leadership capability.

High-performance cultures reap the benefits of implementing their guiding principles. Some of the benefits to the organization and the employees are:

Benefits

To the Organization	*Talent optimization* to execute business strategy today and tomorrow (decreased time to high performance)
	Increased engagement and retention
	Increased organizational capability to adapt to a rapidly changing environment
	Cost savings (developing internal talent is much less expensive than external talent acquisition)
	Increased stock value with viability of future leadership
To Employees	Presents developmental opportunities and support to facilitate high performance
	Focus energy in experiences that tap their passions and skills
	Opportunities to expand knowledge of and exposure within the organization
	Realization of career aspirations

Guiding Principles offer a roadmap for senior leadership and employees to utilize and accomplish their goal of a high-performing culture in the present while building for the future.

Senior Leaders have two primary responsibilities: managing for high performance and managing for accelerated development. This includes an ongoing and dynamic series of job-related interactions between a manager and top talent with the most important activities for manager falling into five key roles:

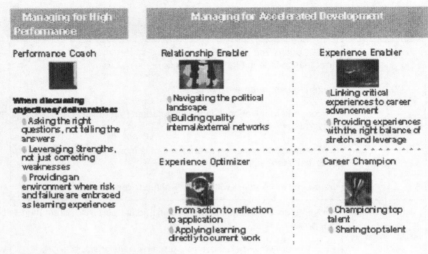

Management's Key Roles

Managing for High Performance	Managing for Accelerated Development	
Performance Coach	Relationship Enabler	Experience Enabler
When discussing objectives/deliverables: ▪ Asking the right questions, not telling the answers ▪ Leveraging Strengths, not just correcting weaknesses ▪ Providing an environment where risk and failure are embraced as learning experiences	▪ Navigating the political landscape ▪ Building quality internal/external networks	▪ Linking critical experiences to career advancement ▪ Providing experiences with the right balance of stretch and leverage
	Experience Optimizer	Career Champion
	▪ From action to reflection to application ▪ Applying learning directly to current work	▪ Championing top talent ▪ Sharing top talent

Note: Based on Corporate Executive Report (2006)

Our vision is to create a high performing organization that consistently delivers outstanding business results through more effective people management.

CEO (APC-2000)

Leadership manages and measures performance to guide and stimulate execution efforts and also to learn from successes as well as failures. The Performance Management process serves as a guide for current efforts. It is composed of two key components — Goals and Capabilities. What sets high performers apart from average performers is that they know clearly what they will achieve and how they will achieve it. Goals capture the "what" and capabilities capture the "how".

Performance coaches include asking the right questions, which enables top talent through the process of discovery to come to their own conclusions/resolve their own issues. This approach enhances learning, motivation, and commitment to the solution/innovation.

Setting Performance Goals

The goal setting process provides the opportunity for a manager and their top talent to focus attention on strategy execution challenges and the results that need to be delivered. Goals serve a number of purposes, including the following:

1. an agreement between you and each of your direct reports,
2. constant reminders and a focus on what is to be achieved and why,
3. a way for employees to be evaluated, and
4. stretch goals take you and your people out of your comfort zone.

Some characteristics of a goal setting process that produces high performance include:

1. A shared understanding exists of current strategic priorities, results expected, and what must be done to achieve the results.
2. Goals are prepared by the employee before meeting face-to-face with the manager to discuss the capabilities required to achieve the goals.
3. Goals and capabilities are finalized in a face-to-face meeting between manager and employee.
4. Feedback sessions are scheduled or agreed to with respect to timing, responsibility for scheduling, etc.
5. A process/mechanism is agreed to with respect to changes in strategic priorities, deliverables, and the impact on goals and capabilities.

The goal setting process can be time consuming, however, it is imperative that both the manager and the employee spend the time and effort needed since everything else follows from this process. Ongoing coaching and feedback, final assessment/reviews, rewards, and in the case of top talent accelerated development opportunities are all dependent on the quality of the goals set and agreed to in the goal setting process.

It is the role of our managers to explain in a transparent and fair way to employees how they are doing, to offer improvement plans and coaching ... and to motivate employees with strong and outstanding performance to continue and to reach the next level of performance.

APC Global Head of HR (2002)

The Performance Management process through effective goal setting, follow-up feedback, and coaching links your top talent's work directly to the organizational goals. The feedback and coaching process enables top talent to excel in their current role. Accelerated development provides the venue for the leader and their top talent to craft a strategy for building stronger capability in areas critical to the organization's as well as their own future growth.

Managing for Accelerated Development for Future Leadership Roles

Accelerated growth opportunities are an important component of managing the top talent process. The purpose is to ensure we merge individual needs with role and business priorities as shown below in Figure 3.1.

To effectively link individual needs with organizational needs, leaders/managers perform four key roles, these roles are based on the Corporate Executive Board (2006).

Philosophy: Merge individual needs with role & business

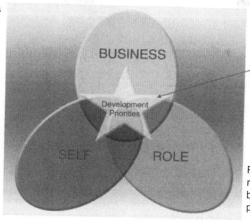

Key business needs, including short and long-term objectives

Impact of individual performance and personal attributes on ability to execute within role and beyond

Immediate actions taken to fully develop business contributions and leadership skills

Participant's role in overall business performance

FIGURE 3.1 Identifying Development Opportunities.

Relationship Enabler

By sharing your knowledge of the organization's landscape you can help top talent navigate networks across the organization. Helping top talent build the right relationships will enhance their learning and create quality internal and external networks.

Experience Enabler

Creating clear connections between critical experiences and career advancement and providing experiences with the right balance of stretch and leverage will accelerate top talent's development.

Experience Optimizer

By providing regular opportunities for top talent to reflect on experience you enhance learning. Top talent should continuously act on and apply what they have learned to their current work.

Career Champion

Acting as a visible, active champion for the long-term development of top talent creates clear links between development and advancement requirements. Building and sharing talent is a critical part of a manager's role.

How to operationalize accelerated development is described below:

Accelerating Development

Purpose:
- Enhance individual and organizational performance
- Place High Potentials into critical positions more quickly

Development is best realized with:
- 70% On-the-Job Experiences/New Job
  (a more challenging job, a developmental task while in current job)
- 20% Relationships -Feedback/observing others
  (role models, coaches, mentors)
- 10% Formal Training -Courses/Readings

Developmental methods work best when *orchestrated together*

Some examples of effective accelerated development experiences are:

Accelerating Development

Examples of components of effective development experiences:
- A challenging task/activity/role (success and failure are possible and visible to others)
- A role of strategic importance with high visibility
- "Take charge" leadership
- Working with new people
- Influencing people vs. direct managerial authority
- Diversity of experiences
- Ongoing Feedback
- Other...

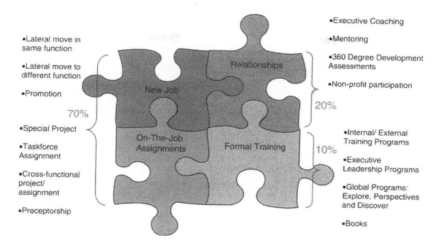

FIGURE 3.2 Development Opportunities.

There are four major categories of developmental opportunities that you and your top talent can discuss and agree on for next steps is shown in Figure 3.2.

High-performance cultures are always on the lookout for matching these developmental opportunities with their top talents needs and the organizations as well.

In structuring your accelerated development strategy and resourcing the plan the Development Cycle displayed in Figure 3.3 offers an approach:

The accelerated development cycle starts where the performance management process provides feedback on current performance and drives the discussion for creating the accelerated development plan. The individual's capability within our strategic priorities and values provide direction for planning accelerated development and provides ways to measure/monitor and assess/act on plans. Top talent will often volunteer to take on tough change initiatives as part of their accelerated development. Formalizing the accelerated development process described above gives both visibility and

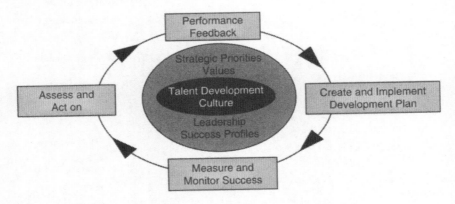

FIGURE 3.3 Ongoing Development Cycle.

credibility to the strategic learning framework that the organization utilizes to execute its strategy and plan for its future.

Strategic Learning can also be a powerful antidote for organizations that have evolved to a point where functions or countries/regions have siloed themselves, where political infighting replaces meritocracy and where the benefits of diversity (nationality, gender, generational, ethnicity, technical specialty, etc.) are ignored. More mature organizations may have more entrenched perspectives or positions in these areas than the emerging multinationals discussed earlier. In either case, strategic learning can be utilized where deep change is needed and active leadership is required to get the change implemented.

Leading Change

Lonza, a specialty chemicals producer since 1897 located on the Rhine River in Northern Europe, was recently showcased as a best practice organization in change management (Simonian, 2007). Lonza approached their most recent reinvention from two perspectives:

1. A rigorous internal review of Lonza's organizational core competence which included a financial analysis and, more importantly, an analysis of their HR capability at the individual and team level. The results of this review identified three new possible directions for Lonza to take.
2. An external confirmation of what they learned internally regarding their capabilities and what path of action they might select

With external confirmation, Lonza's change team identified businesses they should dispose of, how they should restructure the remaining businesses, and what acquisitions made sense going forward. The secret to Lonza's successful reinvention was to involve many internal people in the change discussions, to insist on detailed analysis followed by more discussions, and a written measurable, objectives based plan to guide them as the change process unfolded. Their plan was in one year increments for the next five years. This straightforward formula (with multi-stakeholder involvement) did take longer than if senior management formulated a plan and handed it off to employees for implementation. However, this approach to reinvention encouraged ownership from all employees and significantly decreased employee resistance and hence roll out time was reduced. Additionally, productivity levels remained constant during the reinvention period. Lonza's approach is, unfortunately, not often found in practice. "We know best so please implement the change plan we have formulated" prevails. Of course, the we referenced above is the senior management of the organization.

When asked what keeps you up at night as a business executive, one frequent response is "do we know what must be changed [in our company] to significantly improve business results?" They also add a part two to their response when prodded to expand on their nightmares. What must be changed for us to sustain our company over the long haul?

The fear that short-term change will have a negative impact on longer-term change efforts as well as changes for the long term may hinder current performance are real for these executives. As a result, change efforts may be delayed because to do nothing can seem like a viable alternative rather than choose something that may harm the organization. The good news is that business executives are focusing on both short- and longer-term change issues. The bad news is that many organizations freeze action on needed change because of fear of failure. That is why a critical component for a learning culture is acknowledging failure while supporting the individual and/or team to learn and improve their performance. People get confused when sometimes failure is made public and supported through positive coaching and other times made public and people involved are punished. Consistency in treating failure is critical to the success of change efforts and in particular for reinvention level efforts. Lonza had made changes and some resulted in a significant loss of business. Yet the leadership was able to get employees behind the reinvention, primarily because employees trusted their senior team, but also Lonza brought a focus and discipline to the reinvention process. Employees were confident that they could successfully reinvent themselves not in spite of the failures but because of the way failures were handled.

John Kotter (1995) has written prolifically on why major change efforts often fail in spite of the best intentions of the leadership. Organizational change as a topic of interest is second only to the topic of leadership itself. Rosenzweig (2006) in the Halo Effect cautions us about the stories (case studies) we construct to provide actionable insights from successes or failures. Our insights can be seriously flawed because we frequently shape the story to support our own bias around what is working in an organization and what needs to be changed. Our ability to look at failure and examine its causes and then correct them is very dependent on the context/culture of the organization a person is operating in. If failure teaches you something and you act on what you have learned it can become a positive force for change. However, moving your learning from the individual level to team or organizational level often requires an acceptance by the team or organization of the lessons learned and the change in actions required going forward that become necessary. Poorly developed goals for a strategy, actions that do not enable the goals to be accomplished, seeing only the present and not future states, and perhaps most importantly the social pressure to stay committed to an existing strategy or operating plan that is not delivering results are some possible barriers to leading change. Many projects important to high-performing strategy execution efforts require significant investments by the organizations senior team in their time commitment as well as approving financial and human resources. Changing direction in this context based on learned experience can be a detriment to a person's career. Many organizations, in their Leadership Success Profiles and Talent Management processes, advocate flexibility and willingness to learn and apply new learnings, yet promote people based upon strict adherence to project plans and policy.

With these cautions in mind, change planning and execution efforts are often described as having two primary components:

1. A quantitative analysis documenting the needed change — facts, numbers, data tables, graphs, etc. — current reality in organizational learning terms.
2. The emotional side, i.e. what are or will people be feeling about the change. Both possible negative and positive feelings are identified based upon experience of the change leaders. Ways to maximize positive feelings/ energy around the change and to reduce or minimize the negative aspects are proposed as well.

Strategic Learning utilizes the above techniques but brings a different set of tools to support the major change or reinvention. The Performance Management process and the interactions between managers and their employees discussed above provide the detailed information needed to give structure to the changes in strategy, operations, and culture. The social or emotional side must be handled differently if the organization is to succeed in recreating itself. Dupuy (2002) discusses that making a transfer of knowledge happen presupposes trust between the parties. In organizational level transfers, trust must extend to the senior leadership as well as to teams that the team transferring their knowledge may have little or no direct contact with. In this case, trust almost takes on an element of religious faith. You have to have faith that the rest of the organization will utilize the shared knowledge in a responsible and ethical way and that you as a team or individual will not be less important due to the transference of your knowledge. This is particularly true in Pharma, where patients ingest the product. For many change leaders the ritualism around the change process is almost entirely filled with data analysis, project planning, and setting action steps. Trust and faith in others, especially those not known to the change team, is very rarely spoken about.

APC chose a different way to energize their change leaders. The EC deeply believed that through their product leadership strategy, strategic brands, and global team-based organization that they could reduce cycle time from discovery to patient by 50%. Details about all these beliefs are provided in Chapter 4. As a result of their belief they did not need a huge data book of analogies to support needed change. They did not seek out six sigma teams. They called on their Top 200 business leaders to identify the strategy, operations, and culture changes needed and, then, formed Action Learning Teams (ALTs) to structure and lead the change.

The EC trusted their Top 200 before asking to be trusted. They trusted them to learn what must be changed and then to change it — quickly. They did not seek silver bullet solutions. They wanted solutions that would measurably improve strategy execution. The GHR function had a strong Knowledge Management Consulting team as well as an Organizational Effectiveness function to collaborate with the ALT's and the larger organization. These functions opted to utilize SNA and culture assessments, which when combined, focused the change team in the appropriate area. The APC strategy called for the formation of cross-functional Global Product Teams (GPTs) that focused on launching one product in a therapeutic area for distribution across the world. For example, a GPT was formed for a diabetic drug that would bring relief to millions of patients and improve their quality of life. This global team might include members from R&D, Commercial (Sales/Marketing), Manufacturing, Legal, and Communications/Publications functions depending upon how close the product was to being launched. The 12 key countries would be represented on the team in addition to the functional experts. These GPTs had face-to-face meetings as well as virtual. To support the global team, a global IT system was developed and deployed. This system connected the GPT as well as enabling it to reach out to other GPTs and/or knowledge experts in the organization. A Strategic Learning Community was formed by open and transparent sharing of the team work to date as well as its discussions and findings with non-team experts both in and out of the organization. Universities, strategic alliances with third parties, and Thought Leaders in the therapeutic area were invited to join the Community. More importantly than the IT system were the changes that would be made to the performance management/rewards, talent management, and leadership development processes to support these Strategic Learning Communities. These are discussed in Chapters 4–7. The EC understood the magnitude of the change it was asking its employees to make. The utilization of GPTs and SNA and culture assessments was critical to APC effectively executing its global team-based strategy. Details of APCs definition of SNA are found in Chapter 5 Figures 5.1 and 5.2.

Cross et al. (2007) states "One step toward more effective change lies with better understanding how culture and informal structure influence a change process" (p. 3). The more light that is shed on social network (SN) dynamics, i.e. who communicates/collaborates with whom and who does not the more likely a change plan can be implemented successfully.

By coupling SN dynamics with a deep understanding of the culture and its values you can further improve the chances of a successful change implementation.

Cross also cautions us to be aware of fragmentation points between different teams, functions, or specialties in an organization. For example, engineering may see the culture of their area as rigid and sales may see their culture as empowering.

The power of SNA, including culture analysis, is the shift from a controlling change team to one that is looking for openings to connect the formal and informal structure and their employees to each. The strengths and weaknesses of the existing strategy, operations, and culture can become open for discussion. Once dialogue is started it is often not possible to stop it. The skill of the change team is critical here or action will not follow words. These dialogues have the power to self-heal long-standing differences between teams, functions, and geographies. The change team can often exit, because the people who must change have taken over the initiative, internalized it, and are moving to implementation.

Finally, a well-executed SNA and culture analysis will reveal enemies to the change needed. Dialogue and conflict resolution may not be able to overcome the negativity to the change generated by these enemies. Some change teams act like Special Operations teams in the Military. They are trained, even under the most chaotic circumstances, to quickly identify the enemies of their mission and eliminate them. In corporations, enemies can be transferred or taken off teams if needed.

Learning may be difficult but leading a successful change initiative is much more difficult. Balancing the need for quantitative data and analysis and the more qualitative SN aspects of a major change initiative defy a formulaic approach to strategizing and implementing the change initiative. Yet many organizations require just such a formulaic approach from their change agents. Well-detailed project management plans documenting the changes needed frequently consume much of the time and energy an organization can allot to the changes needed.

Organizations are encouraged to institutionalize best practices, freeze them into place, focus on execution, stick to their knitting, increase predictability, and get processes under control. These ideas establish stability as the key to performance. As a result, organizations are built to support enduring values, stable strategies, and bureaucratic structures, not to change.

Lawler and Worley (2006)

Part II discusses in greater detail how APC was formed, how its strategy emerged and how GHR and R&D HR utilized strategic learning and leading change principles to build a new kind of pharma organization.

References

Agins, T. *The End of the Fashion Industry: How Marketing Changed the Clothing Business Forever.* New York: HarperCollins, 1999.

Corporate Executive Board. *Developing Senior Leaders Who Develop Rising Stars.* Washington, DC, 2006.

Cross R., Johnson-Cramer, M., and Parise, S. *Managing Change Through Networks and Values: How a Relational View of Culture Can Facilitate Large-Scale Change,* The Network Roundtable at the University of Virginia, 2007.

Dupuy, F. *The Chemistry of Change: Problems, Phases and Strategy.* New York: Palgrave, 2002.

Engardio, P. "Emerging Giants." *Business Week Cover Story* (2006, July 31): 41–48.

Kotter, J. P. "Leading Change: Why Transformation Efforts Fail." *Harvard Business Review,* March–April, Boston, MA, 1995.

Lawler, E. E., and Worley, C. G. *Built to Change: How to Achieve Sustained Organizational Effectiveness.* San Francisco, CA: Jossey-Bass, 2006.

Mezirow, J. *Transformative Dimensions of Adult Learning.* SanFrancisco, CA: Jossey-Bass, 1991.

Rosenzweig, P. *The Halo Effect: … and the Eight Other Business Delusions that Deceive Managers.* Switzerland: IMD, Lausanne, 2006.

Schon, D. A. *Educating the Reflective Practitioner.* San Francisco, CA: Jossey-Bass, 1987.

Simonian, H. "From Reaction to Reinvention. Financial Times." *Business Life-Change Management*, January, 27, London, England, 2007.

Watkins, K. E., and Marsick, V. J. *Sculpting the Learning Organization: Lessons in the Art and Science of Systemic Change.* San Francisco, CA: Jossey-Bass, 1993.

II

REINVENTING PHARMA

APC, a European-based Pharma company committed to building a global team-based organization, was determined to reinvent the Pharma business model. This would be accomplished by embedding a strategic learning and leading culture change capability throughout their organization. Chapter 4 discusses the Executive Committee's strategy to transform their company from a Country-based strategy model to a global team-based organization. The role of HR as a strategic business partner is explored as well as the use of global Action Learning Teams. Chapter 5 explores how the globalization of the R&D function would lead to the entire organization becoming a global team-based organization. R&D would utilize strategic learning principles and tools such as the One Page Strategy, Communities of Practice, Champions of Knowledge Sharing Awards Program, Knowledge expertise Locator technologies, and a high-performing global team process to institutionalize the changes needed. Chapter 6 discusses how APC went about building its leadership capability and pipeline across the entire organization. Their leadership profile is presented and its use became the foundation for APC's performance management, talent management, and leadership development initiatives. Chapter 7 explores the culture change needed for APC to successfully move to a global team-based organization. The strategy and tactics of R&D and HR as the culture change agents including their use of strategic learning principles and communications to implement the change plan are explored.

4

Globalizing Pharma — The APC Way

A dream of every HR executive is to have their function seen by business leaders as not just HR but strategic HR — HR as a business partner — not just at the EC table — but a fully participating member of the EC. Not only being a member but also a coach to the executives in charge. In 2000, as APC's first year as a merged organization started, HR had its hands full.

APC (a European based Pharma) was fortunate indeed. Since its formation in late 1999 from two medium-sized, mediocre-performing Pharma companies, it had an aura of excitement and mystery about it. Recruiting new talent into the organization, while challenging because of the sheer number of people needed, was not especially difficult. There was lots of buzz about APC both internally as well as externally about this new kind of Pharma Company and how it intended to globalize the Pharma business. Existing employees unashamedly talked about the excitement they felt in being part of a new kind of Pharma Company. A company that was truly global in its strategy, vision, and operating processes. APC employees prided themselves on creating a global high performing team based (GHPT) organization -not using teams as a way to execute strategy — but global teams were the strategy. Of course the highly competitive nature of the modern Pharma landscape required that these teams be nothing less than high performing.

Everyone in APC knew it would be difficult to "pull off". The Pharma business was a complex business with a long timeline from molecule discovery to launch of a new product. It was risky during the discovery to launch time period since very few molecules ever made it to pharmaceutical products. The risk did not end at launch — in fact it just got a whole lot more serious. Competitor's products, shorter patent protection periods, and pricing pressures from governments and health care providers to lower prices all made for a tough competitive market space. In addition, a number of products were now coming under scrutiny about their long-term safety as well as efficacy. In addition to the external challenges of the Pharma business, there would be very difficult problems to be solved internally. Most Pharma executives had gained their experience in highly regionalized/country structured Pharma companies. Most of these companies utilized teams at times to deliver specific project/initiative results. Few, if any, had global teams as the core of their strategy and tactics — much less high-performing teams. The EC would have to convince the many smart people populating APC, as well as those joining the company, that their way was the way to run the next generation of Pharma companies.

The EC Structures Itself for Success

The EC, from the very beginning, designed a reporting structure that would ensure effective strategy execution. The EC consisted of the Chairman/CEO (CEO) and his direct reports. Only global function heads reported to the CEO. The intent was clear-strategy and its execution would be at the global level and not at the country head/general manager level as in many other Pharma companies. Specific functions are given in Figure 4.1.

These functions covered all key areas needed to effectively plan, communicate, and execute strategy. Country Heads reported into a global function head. In addition to global functional reporting relationships, the EC assigned global

FIGURE 4.1 APC Global Functions.

budget as well as profit and loss (P&L) responsibility to the global function heads that in turn assigned similar responsibilities to their GPTs.

Each global function head was expected to build GHPTs within their respective functions as well as across functions. The mandate was clear. Global teams within a function and then across functions were the core of the APC strategy. Specifically the Commercial, Industrial, and R&D functions would set shared cross-functional goals at the global function head level and then cascade them to their direct reports who in turn would cascade them to their direct reports, and so on down through the organization. Most cross-functional goal setting at each level would take place in face-to-face meetings which required a great deal of travel for team members. Meetings would be held in different countries so that all participants would be equally traveling to ensure fairness.

Shared global goals across the functions would not be sufficient to make APC's vision of a global Pharma company a reality. APC had hundreds of products sold in a large number of countries. APC would have to change that quickly. The EC adopted a strategic brand focus to complement the GHPT concept. This focus emphasized discovering and launching innovative drugs in therapeutic areas with high medical needs and large patient populations. A long-term goal was to have a number of these innovative products — a portfolio approach — for each of the disease group areas that APC determined to be a major player. APC went on to define more specifically what a strategic brand meant in terms of sales dollars and sales presence, i.e. countries. A yearly sale of 1 billion dollars with presence in the 12 core countries was their goal. Each product was reviewed to make a determination if it fit the strategic brand concept going forward. Those products not fitting the definition were sold to other companies where possible or discontinued.

The APC Value Proposition

The organization must work like an orchestra ... different processes from discovery to development to manufacture to marketing to sales ... must be in sync ... The organization must be fluid ... made up of technical teams and ad hoc teams ... our challenge is to ensure that the organization's structure does not interfere with natural team structures.

CEO APC Executive Offsite (2000)

The engine of the organization was GHPTs, unfettered by organizational structure and burdensome bureaucracy. The APC operating model was to be a unique blend of a product leadership strategy and a people strategy that would revolutionize the Pharma industry sector. Some said a "grand plan", others said absolutely a crazy way to run a company. A product leadership company focuses on product innovation first and then very quickly and effectively product development and market exploitation. A networked flexible organizational structure keeps people close to the ever-changing environment. Couple such a structure with a result-driven performance and rewards management system that rewards successes and encourages experimentation without punishing failures leads to a culture that creates the future as the work of the present is completed. The key components of a product leadership company are:

- Breakthrough vision and product innovation,
- Ambitious and clear targets,
- Balance between flexibility and discipline,
- People of superior talent with a thirst for problem-solving, and
- A distaste for bureaucracy.

Product Leadership organizations are also known for the operating principles they espouse:

- Business structures do not interfere with high-performance teams,
- Strictly follow procedures where the payoffs are the greatest — e.g. Product development,
- Balance creativity and the concerns of fiscal practicality,
- Innovate the next generation of products while simultaneously prolonging the life of existing products, and
- Insist on excellence as the standard in marketing and selling.

The EC tirelessly communicated and modeled the key elements of their people strategy. It was all about believing in their people — trusting them to communicate the strategy, align their team to it, and execute the strategy at high-performing levels.

The foremost resource for any organization is recruiting, developing, and rewarding people of superior talent. Fielding the best team is the standard to be attained. It is not enough for an individual to be more effective than their counterpart in the competitions workforce. The teams must be better across the board if the organization is to be in and stay in the top tier of its industry. Leading and managing such a workforce is critical to the success of the enterprise. Finding the best and brightest employees often means encouraging the gadflies and concept champions. Leaders/managers are often charged with moving valuable people to projects that generate the most value for the organization, where roles are fuzzy, stature non-existent, and extraordinary levels of ambiguity exist. Knowledge is often created and transferred through informal mechanisms such as coaching and mentoring rather than formal data/knowledge transfer systems. Throughout the entire value creation process, top-notch individual contributors must always be focused on the team — in APC's case global teams where differences are easier to list than synergies, where time and distance separations make accomplishing simple tasks complex and difficult ones feats of extraordinary persistence and courage. APC's leadership was often heard saying, "The highest form of recognition for talented people is selection for the next even more challenging assignment ... star players are always anxious to learn what's over the horizon". Star players who are team players are every leader's dream especially where global teams are the strategy.

The EC realized early on that globalizing the HR function was critical to their success in creating their global Pharma company. In fact, HR would have to get global at least one step ahead of all the other functions if they were to succeed over the short term. It would also be impossible to sustain the global organization over the long term without the support of the HR function. It was the EC that early on embraced the Global Head of HR as a strategic business partner and coach.

The Head of GHR was charged with the transformation of the regional/country-based HR organizations that APC started with at their integration in the late 1990s to a global team-based organization that modeled the way for the commercial, industrial, research/development, and support functions.

Transforming HR

Early on in 2000, it was clear to the CEO that the HR function was not globalizing fast enough for the organization to change itself from a regionally centered Country Manager structured organization to a global team-based organization. Speed was critical — where was the HR function's sense of urgency? Talent Management, performance and rewards management, and leadership development all needed to be globalized now. It also became clear the current head of HR would have to replaced, a new one selected and an interim plan developed to globalize the company's key HR practices during the integration phase of the merger. Valuable time would be lost if the integration period passed without these key HR practices going global.

The CEO wasted no time in reaching out to his network for a global Head of HR who would be up to the challenges ahead. While the details of bringing in this HR executive were being worked out, an interim strategy to build the high-performing team-based culture was operationalized. It was also abundantly clear to the EC that the capability level of the functional and country HR departments would have to be raised significantly. There were pockets of outstanding talented HR professionals throughout the organization. The goal was to move from these pockets to having all HR professionals be at a high level of capability.

The Early Days

The EC, with full support from global HR, used 2000 to their advantage as HR prepared itself for the challenges ahead. The CEO started the integration off with a meeting of the Top 200 business leaders across the organization that focused on identifying the critical issues APC faced with particular emphasis on the new company's values and the global teaming concept. As a result of the meeting a number of ALTs were formed around a range of issues such as differentiating performance and then rewards, identifying high potentials earlier than prior Talent Management processes, developing leaders as teachers and coaches, and significantly improving the efficiency and effectiveness of the R&D function. These issues needed immediate solutions if APC was to successfully execute its strategy. The timeline was quite short — in fact most employees described it as very aggressive but necessary. You could feel the passion in their voices as they described their teams, the work they did and the results they achieved.

The ALTs were cross-functional as well as regional teams. In addition the team leaders reached beyond the Top 200 to staff the teams. In all there were approximately 15 teams each focused on an integration issue around values, strategy, people, or processes. Perhaps the most important ALT was the one formed around the role HR would play in the organization going forward. What strategy should HR come forward with? What structure would add the most value to line leaders and employees? What was right about HR now and what was not and needed to be fixed? Finally, what needed to be done immediately by HR for APC to move its global strategy ahead?

As stated above the ALTs were designed to quickly define their issue, organize themselves, provide several alternative solutions for the EC to consider with a recommendation, and finally to identify a champion who would be able to influence the organization's employees to implement the solution globally and locally. Their mandate was to gather internal data/information in the area of their charter as well as to benchmark external best practices. The ALT would then combine their findings and prepare a summary report including recommendations to their EC sponsor. They would then be scheduled to present their findings to the entire EC. The EC set aside one of its bi-weekly meetings for all ALTs to present. The EC would either approve in whole or part an ALTs recommendations. In some cases, the EC would defer a decision until more data was provided or they needed to think more about the issue and the proposed solutions. In any case they would decide to move ahead or not within two weeks which was their next scheduled meeting. Implementation teams would be formed immediately upon approval of the recommendations by the EC. At least one person from the original ALT would be on the implementation team to support the implementation team's work going forward. This person would be a resource providing context and depth on the thinking and discussions the original team had — explaining in some detail why and how the team came up with its recommendation.

The EC was also concerned about developing its leadership talent. They agreed that in the first year of the integration there would be little time to send people to traditional leadership development programs or customize one for the new organization. Everyone was working way too hard to spend time in this area. The EC knew it also could not completely ignore the development of their leadership talent especially their high-potential talent. People would leave the organization if senior leadership did not visibly support and participate in developing their leadership talent globally and locally. As a result the EC working with HR leadership and an outside consultancy came up with an interim leadership development plan that fit the organization's needs until a more formal one could be designed and agreed to. First, leadership development would be embedded into their yearly meeting of the Top 200. Well-known external business leaders would be brought in to work with the group in building awareness and skill in selected areas. For example, Jack Welch was brought in to discuss creating the boundary-less organization and differentiating performance and rewards. Second, each ALT would have an external coach who would provide in team just in time leadership development based on the needs of the team as they were executing their mandate.

In parallel to the above development activities, HR worked on designing a LSP specific to the new organization. This profile would become the foundation of the Talent Management, Performance Management, and Leadership Development strategies as APC moved rapidly to transform itself. A 360-degree assessment tool was designed after the senior leadership of the organization approved the LSP. The EC then underwent a 360 assessment, debriefed by an outside coach, and made agreements in-group as to their individual development plans. This went quickly through the organization reinforcing the EC's commitment to the LSP, developing leadership skills critical to APC and most importantly the transparency with which they did their 360 and then shared development plans.

The ALTs were critical in rapidly moving APC to discuss and agree on strategies, shared terminology, processes, and policies around performance management, rewards, leadership development, and talent management. These teams were also critical in defining the global team-based organization.

As HR began transforming itself in 2000, they also spearheaded several other initiatives that would be needed. A global employee satisfaction/engagement survey was designed and deployed in early spring of 2000. Many executives, including the EC, were apprehensive about the results. Did they really want to know how their people were thinking and feeling about the new organization and by inference their leadership of it to date? Overall the results were good considering the turbulence in the merging of the two companies. It was also clear that a number of things would need to change if the global team-based organization was to take hold. The survey data clearly showed that the organization was very heavily siloed by function and/or country. Neither of which was good for globalizing the organization. In fact the combined organization was much more siloed than either predecessor companies! It seemed that people were digging in to preserve the old country/functional model. This would need to be addressed quickly. Also the survey data was clear — employees felt that policies and procedures were not fairly and consistently being applied across the organization. Employees thought that who you worked for and where you worked were more important in how you were treated than what you delivered. These were not positive conditions for building a global organization.

Out of the fog of integration, it became clear that HR would be an important strategic player and that the speed and quality with which HR could transform itself would be one of the critical success factors for APC.

HR Steps Up Its Transformation

As the efforts of the EC, Top 200, Global HR (GHR), and the ALTs moved the organization forward in 2000, GHR was busy designing and implementing its structure and value proposition.

The new Head of GHR, who knew a number of EC members prior to joining APC, immediately, went to work. He informed the EC of his intent in creating the new GHR structure.

The GHR as well as global function and country HR organization structures must mirror the business structure of APC ... we must organize in a way that leverages our global functional organization while recognizing our need for local operations.

EC meeting (2000)

He saw three primary roles in HR:

1. Corporate — charged with setting overall HR strategy for APC and the primary contact with the EC. In developing people strategies, processes, and tools, Corporate would act as a Center of Excellence collaborating with global HR functions as well as country HR organizations.
2. Global functions — senior HR executives working directly with global function Heads who were direct reports to the CEO as described above. Each global function would have a dedicated HR department, working with Corporate HR to design and deploy HR initiatives as needed. HR professionals were expected to act as business partners on the functional leadership teams.
3. Country/Region — senior HR executives focused on operational excellence on the ground. These HR organizations would need to interact in a collaborative way with global functional HR as well as Corporate HR. HR professionals were expected to act as business partners on country/regional leadership teams.

This structure parallels the business structure described as "the global matrix" by APC's business leaders and employees. All three roles shared the responsibility of developing the going forward HR strategy into 2001 and beyond. Their shared goal was to design and deploy HR initiatives and programs all of which aligned to the strategic business objectives of the EC. While having the Head of GHR, as a respected and active member of the EC did not insure alignment, it was at least in the realm of the possible to accomplish. Two challenges surfaced immediately after deploying the new GHR organization in mid-2000:

1. Communication, and hence coordinated actions, between Corporate, Functional, and Country/Regional HR organizations were strained at best and non-existent in most cases. Informal communications would not be effective in combating the lack of or strained communications that were due primarily to the complexity of the organizations global matrix structure.
2. The HR professional's capability to assume a strategic business partner role on their respective business leadership team was not at a level needed in most cases. HR capability dropped significantly after the senior HR executive level leaving a large gap in delivering strategic HR thinking and actions. This capability gap would impact Corporate HRs delivering on its mandates from the EC.

Both of these would need immediate action and solutions. The Head of GHR formed a human resource council (HRC). The HRC was composed of the senior most GR executive in the global functions as well the countries/regions. Their mandate was to meet monthly — face-to-face — to discuss and agree on the HR strategy, policies, processes, and initiatives needed to create the global team-based organization in their respective part of the organization. Specific action plans would be formulated and status would be reported monthly. To assist the HRC in meeting its mandate, a global management development committee (GMDC) was formed. The GMDC would meet — face-to-face — quarterly and more if needed. The members of this committee were direct reports of the HRC members. Both the HRC and the GMDC had approximately 15 members. Within six months there was a notable improvement in the quality of communication as well as coordinated action by HR. The functional and country/regional business leadership teams were electronically surveyed or "pulsed" to evaluate how well HR was performing in delivering its value proposition. While communications improved, as 2001 closed feedback from the business leaders about HRs capability to act as a business partner further declined as more strategic HR initiatives were being rolled out. Something needed to be done immediately but a business reorganization would put this on hold until late in 2002.

APC Reorganizes

The EC in 2000 decided that APC would need to become a "pure Pharma" company if it was to realize its vision of becoming a GHPT-based organization. The Supervisory Board gave its consent for management to divest all non-Pharma businesses and focus all its efforts on pharmaceuticals. The goal was to focus on Pharma and to grow the company "through innovative, patented prescription drugs". The investment community recognized the future value of the APC strategy. APC share price rose 60 percent in 2000, which clearly outperformed the European, and U.S. stock indices.

In spring of 2002, with the divestitures of non-Pharma businesses completed, APC streamlined its senior management structure. The EC was disbanded and a Management Board was elected to run the company on a day-to-day basis. There were management personnel changes. There were personnel changes, e.g. the CEO of the EC became Co-Vice Chairman and Chief Operating Officer, a new Chairman/CEO was installed. Most importantly, the Head of Global HR was replaced — not for poor performance because his GHR strategy and execution were moving the organization ahead. In fact his efforts had substantially improved the reputation of the HR function by most measures. The Management Board decided that to further expedite the transformation of the HR function a senior line executive would be placed in charge and be a full member of the Management Board. The existing Head of GHR was offered a position on the Operating Management Committee comprised of the direct reports of the Management Board. He declined and left the organization. A loss for sure but not a showstopper as 2002 and 2003 would prove. The Management Board like the EC before it was composed of the global function heads. The Operating Management Committee was composed of senior function heads as well as country/region heads. For all practical purposes global function heads were still running APC. The APC vision of creating a GHPT-based organization was still the organization of choice.

More importantly than the technical business leadership structure and related strategies was the "Building on People" philosophy that emerged in 2000 from the efforts of the EC, GHR, and the ALTs and was continued by the newly elected Management Board and Operating Management Committee. The cornerstones of this philosophy were all employees living a shared set of values, focusing on superior individual and team performance, differentiated rewards for high performers, developing leaders at all levels of the organization, and promotion opportunities that were second to none in the industry. The newly elected Head of GHR would put his stamp on the function for sure. His last assignment was Country Head of one of APC's largest and most productive countries. He was a seasoned business executive who had faced implementing people strategies in turbulent times both at the country level and at a global level. In addition, he was an extraordinary team builder and a leader who could set a vision and motivate people to work towards the vision. It was a great time to be in HR.

Global HR Reorganizes

To sustain our value we have to get better and better ...
compete with our own success.

Newly Appointed Head, GHR (Summer 2002)

APC had committed to building a GHPT-based organization that was a product leader in Pharma. The measure would be out performing the competition in discovering and bringing to market the most innovative pharmaceuticals in areas that had high medical needs and large patient populations. GHR would continue to support this value proposition. The Head of GHR called for a global offsite later in 2002. Over 100 of the organizations senior HR executives would gather for three days to review HRs progress to date in transforming itself and to renew their spirit for creating an even more effective and efficient HR organization. Attendees represented the corporate, function, and country/regional HR organizations.

The offsite started off by asking each participant to think about and prepare responses to the following questions:

- How do we (HR) contribute to the APC value proposition?
- Are we delivering more value this year than last? Why or why not?
- How can we work differently together to contribute more value?
- What stands in the way of doing better? How can we overcome the obstacles?

These were tough questions to ask and answer. The offsite went well beyond the HRC and GMDC to define the present state and come up with solutions to building a more effective HR organization at all levels. The prior Head of GHR had planned such a conference to gather more feedback from more people to accelerate the HR transformation. APC, however, had put in a travel ban after the 9/11 tragedies in the US. The HRC meetings continued to be face-to-face almost immediately after 9/11 with the GMDC starting face-to-face in March of 2002. The offsite participants, working in small teams, immediately generated a number of ideas that would accelerate the transformation of HR across the board. The Chairman of the Management Board/EC as well as other EC members came to the meeting to emphasize the importance of HR succeeding in its transformation. In addition, line executives from all functions joined in the offsite to work on the teams as well in plenary sessions for all to hear the output of the teams. This ensured that the changes to HR strategy, policies, processes, initiatives, and tools would be relevant and aligned to the business leaders needs.

As the offsite progressed, many of the ideas were discussed and prioritized with help of the attending line executives. The challenges for HR emerged during the last hours of the offsite:

1. Develop organization design expertise to build structures within APC that
   a. maximize creativity and innovation;
   b. ensure ownership and accountability;
   c. minimize bureaucracy; and
   d. foster teaming and networking.
2. Assist leaders in the design of fluid structures where
   a. people can change focus and direction quickly;
   b. systems are self correcting — information on external and internal performance is fed back quickly; and
   c. resources are managed to produce what the market needs but also enables the organization to stay ahead of the market.
3. Become excellent talent management consultants and coaches
   a. understand the environment and assist managers in selecting/developing people who embrace change, thrive in a team-based networked/flexible environment.
4. Excel at performance managemen
   a. work with leadership to develop metrics that encourage behaviors needed to sustain product leadership;
   b. work with the organization to set appropriate goals, milestones, and activities;
   c. provide expertise in coaching to maximize performance; and
   d. design flexible reward and recognition programs.

Ensure that highly developed coaching skills were present throughout the leadership and management ranks to transfer the organization's knowledge/intelligence throughout.

Finally, HR must act as agents of change in assisting the organization in building the culture needed to deliver results to its customers, employees, and shareholders.

The Head of GHR closed the conference by reiterating the APC HR Vision/Value proposition:

> *APC HR creates value by working with its customers to attract, develop, and retain a pipeline of top talent and key contributors who will build a high performing team based culture.*

He went on to emphasize "we in HR see ourselves as strategic business partners to the APC business operations". Then he stated "our goals for 2003 must be to improve our global Talent Management, Performance Management, and Leadership Development strategies and processes. We as HR must be committed to building our individual capabilities to meet the challenges ahead". True to its heritage APC formed ALT like teams around the areas described above. There were eight teams in all. Critical to HR delivering on its promises was the speed and effectiveness with which it could improve its people's capabilities.

Building HR Capabilities

As the Head of GHR was fond of doing, he started off this conference with a question for the participants to think about, discuss, network internally and externally for best practices, and to come back to the HRC with a strong recommendation within 90 days of the end of the conference. A very large deliverable considering the team, like many teams in APC, this team was globally dispersed with varying levels of expertise in the area and time to devote to the team's objective. This team was viewed as the most important team coming out of the conference. Its recommendations would be the model for other functions to build their capability profiles as well as a roadmap for building an exciting career within HR. This team was the only team that had two HRC members as sponsors. The team would be able to tap into their considerable expertise in the area of HR capabilities.

The question he posed was:

What HR capabilities profile will be required to effectively deliver the HR value proposition to our internal customers, and how would we achieve excellence against this capability profile.

The team went right to work — time was of the essence. Like any team of diverse individuals, this team struggled to form itself into a high-performing team. It seemed like the storming would never end. Discussion after discussion went on for the first two meetings — meetings that were a full day's travel to and from for team members in addition to the time spent in the team meeting itself. A breakthrough occurred thanks to the two HRC co-sponsors. Both were well respected for their openness to new ideas and being able to influence senior management to accept the recommendations of employees of changes needed to strategy, operations, or culture. They were role models of strategic learning and leading change. They were fearless in reflecting on successes and failures and modifying actions going forward. They sensed the team was struggling and took time out of their already full work schedules to travel to the third team meeting. This did the trick — they helped focus the team on its shared goals as well as arriving at a team process that encouraged dialogue but also brought dialogue to a decision point. The team quickly split the deliverable into sub-team assignments — e.g. one sub-team did external benchmarking with a number of companies in and out of the Pharma industry to identify best practices in HR service delivery and the capabilities needed to achieve such results. The team delivered on time on budget and at a quality that drew praise from the Head of GHR as well as the Management Board.

FIGURE 4.2 HR Capability Profile.

The team identified ten capabilities that were clustered in four categories found in Figure 4.2.

While all four categories were important it was felt by the HRC and GMDC that Business Acumen would need the most development for the majority of HR professionals. Many had not studied business in their professional schooling and the more junior HR people were not being exposed to the line management/leadership in their function or country. To further support the capabilities profile, the team recommended the "3 C's" model:

1. Credibility
   a. Doing what we say we will do.
   b. Demonstrating the highest levels of integrity.

2. Competence
   a. Continually upgrading business and functional skills.
   b. Broadening your professional toolkit to address organizational needs, e.g. HR Generalists becoming skilled at Organizational Effectiveness Capabilities.
   c. Venture outside the organization and industry to seek out best practices.
   d. Share your knowledge with others — teach and coach and mentor.
3. Courage
   a. Challenge current processes in and out of HR.
   b. Push for continuous improvement.
   c. Take risks.

The team also felt strongly about placing APC's values as the center of the capabilities profile. Many on the team remembered the CEO way back at the start of APC in early 2000 stating.

If they [our values] are reflected in our behavior, if they are reflected in how we reward people, how we promote them, if they are reflected in the new employees we bring into the company, then eventually, step by step, over time the only people that are left are the ones that have these values ... these values will shape the culture ... these are the values that will lead to a high performing team based company.

The rollout plan was simple and quickly implemented. It was now the beginning of the second quarter of 2003. The Head of GHR would send out to all HR executives a rollout kit for their area. The kit would contain sample communication material for them to translate into their country's language, a computerized 360-assessment form, and an individual development toolkit for each HR professional to use in setting development goals for one or more of the capabilities. The HRC and GMDC would assist in the implementation at the function and country levels. Immediate usage was encouraged, i.e. not waiting until the year-end performance review cycle to set development goals. There was no time to waste in improving each HR professional's capability.

Phase 2 of the rollout was to take place in October of 2003. In addition to the HR Capability profile, feedback from line management indicated that functional and country HR personnel needed to have a deeper knowledge of Talent Management, Performance and Rewards Management, and Individual Development Planning. In addition, since many HR professionals needed Business Acumen improvement, they should also be trained on the characteristics of high-performing organizations and how the people strategy contributes. The GMDC took primary responsibility for developing the training materials and design of the workshop. One workshop was run in the US that also covered Canada and Latin America with a second workshop in Europe that covered Asia as well. In all 60 senior HR professionals were trained to deliver training to their HR personnel as well as to line managers on a "just in time" basis. Figure 4.3 shows the respective global core HR processes and the timing of the training for each process. A library of materials was prepared and available on line for HR to use with their internal clients. Materials were provided as modules or in topic libraries for customizing the training to fit functional or country needs.

As 2003 closed, GHR re-communicated its priorities for 2004. They recommitted to working with senior and line management to assist them in fielding the best team — the right players in the right place with the right skills to execute the strategy better than the competition. GHR also reiterated its commitment to improving performance and Rewards Management, Talent Management, and Leadership Development over the upcoming year. The future looked very bright indeed for APC and for GHR. Company results were good considering the pressures on the industry and stock prices. The pipeline held promise and global teams were taking hold in all functional areas of the company.

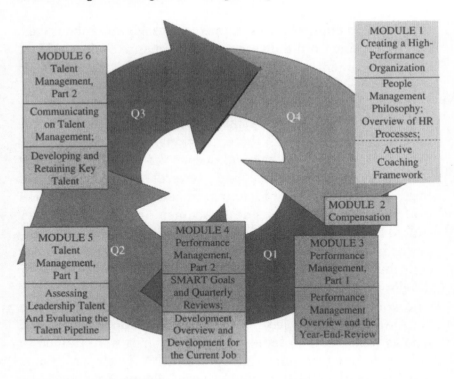

FIGURE 4.3 Manager Workshops by Quarter.

The HR Report Card

The HR organization, since 2000, had made enormous progress in transforming itself from a regional-based strategy and structure to a global functional and country/regional-based matrix organization. Over 2000 and 2001 HR had designed and deployed a number of initiatives all aimed at supporting the EC in building the GHPT-based organization that was the centerpiece of its strategy. In 2002, HR restructured itself based on direct feedback from the EC, Management Board, the Top 200, line management, and from global survey results of all employees. HR had sought feedback and used this feedback to continuously improve its performance. HR had focused on Talent Management, Performance and Rewards Management, and Leadership Development.

As 2003 started, HR received additional feedback on needed changes to the people strategy:

1. Talent Management
   a. There were too few high potentials identified given the size of the company.
   b. Gaps in the talent pipeline for some critical positions.
   c. A number of smaller countries as well as lower level management personnel not yet in the Talent Pipeline.
   d. Development plans for High Potentials are often missing.
   e. Cross-functional/cross-geography moves rare.
2. Performance Management
   a. Top performers not always in critical positions.
   b. Management of poor performers needs to be a priority.
   c. Dual career path for highly valued technical resources not consistent or completely rolled out in functions and regions.
3. Leadership Development
   a. Need a program for senior leaders —VPs and above that mirrors the programs for managers and directors — cross-functional cross-regional teams working on strategy execution issues facing APC.

Finally, HRs stated goal had been to flawlessly execute global processes. Feedback indicated that HR was doing well but not world class. It would need to step up its game in this area. A number of people internal to HR also noted some improvements that were needed. In 2000 and 2001 the HRC and GMDC meetings were like the Wild West. There was lots of brawling and noise but little agreement on the globalization of core HR processes. Most senior HR professionals, like line leadership, were experienced in a Country-managed Pharma company and not a global team-based organization strategy and structure. As a result, many HR professionals preferred to stay with their Countries programs and policies and not adopt global ones they were unsure of. People dreaded presenting at these meetings since emotions often ran high and respect for the presenter was often missing. However, they did not give up on each other. A few stepped up and courageously led the way to a kinder gentler yet effective HR organization. These few individuals, like the two co-team sponsors discussed above, were role models for strategic learning and leading deep change at the culture level. Employees trusted them to be innovative but also forthright in the change required to implement the global strategy. Employees also felt that they would be treated fairly as they moved from the old strategy and ways of doing things to the new strategy and operations. These few courageous individuals instilled a sense of community and membership in the new organization, i.e. a sense of belonging and higher purpose for all. By 2003, major differences had been worked out and the HRC and GMDC separately and together were working collaboratively. When differences arose, respectful dialogue was the order of the day. Those who were there from the beginning could see the level of transformation accomplished over such a short time period. Those who were not there from the beginning could not believe the stories of the "old days". HR was committed to responding to the feedback and looked to ALT like teams to partner with. Customers and HR personnel would be working together to solve the issues.

One lingering feedback from the beginning from the line leadership was the need to connect all the core HR processes for them — to take a systems view. HR addressed this in Phase 2 of the training of HR personnel so they could train line management who in turn would train their people.

Figure 4.4, with supporting materials, was developed by GHR and utilized by functional and country/regional HR to improve line management's systemic understanding of the core processes. By most accounts this one slide made a major contribution in this area. In addition, a portal was designed and deployed for all employees to visit. The portal had detailed information about Talent Management, Performance/Rewards Management,

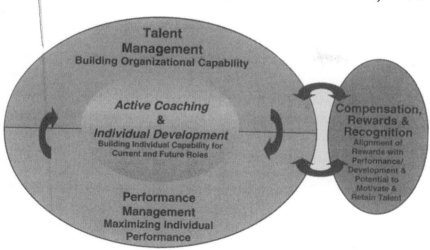

FIGURE 4.4 How the Processes Fit Together to Create a High-Performance Organization.

and Leadership Resources. Philosophy, guidelines, policies, leadership training, forms, e-learning modules, job aids, and tools were available for use. The portal proved to be a great electronic ambassador for explaining the global team-based strategy and the support available from HR. Key opinion leaders from all global functions and countries were briefed face-to-face and their support obtained before the release of the portal. EC representation from all global functions had been part of the design plan for the portal. The EC and key opinion leaders both gave HR their unconditional support, yet another visible sign of the organization's leadership's commitment to developing its people.

Lessons Learned

APC was determined to globalize the Pharma industry by building a GHPT-based organization that also provided an environment that drew people to it and kept them there. There was magic in the air for sure and also some growing pains along the way. Some lessons learned:

1. Senior executives were replaced when needed. There were three Heads of HR in four years. Other global functions experienced this as well. The key to successfully doing this was senior managements' requirement that the new executive not dismantle what was already built. The newly appointed executive was expected to fix problem areas identified. This mitigated the feeling that there would be a constant stream of "programs du jour" as the executive took charge. Employees when surveyed indicated an understanding of the nature of the changes needed and the reasoning behind the change. By not dismantling prior change efforts a sense of connection between the past, present, and the move to the future state was achieved. In addition specific goal setting and tracking by the CEO and his team was critical and their feedback acted on, if the new executive was to succeed. Employees saw a powerful commitment of the senior team to work together collaboratively and not act as independent committee members interested only in their functional area's responsibilities in delivering high-performing strategy execution.

2. The senior teams at the global, functional, and country/ regional level were visible and were continuously communicating, using multiple media, the strategy, the results, and the changes needed to be made — they effectively modeled the way regarding needed changes. This process ensured a sharing of individual, team, and functional level learnings across the entire organization. As a result new internal alliances formed across functions and regions which resulted in the organization more quickly implementing change. In essence this became a model for building the Social Networks needed to create the global team-based strategy.

3. Management at all levels looked for innovative ways to celebrate teams and individuals as well — it is possible but takes incredible amounts of time and effort by management. Employees saw other employees visibly recognized for their efforts and a healthy competitive spirit arose within the organization as a result. When surveyed, employees indicated that this was time well spent by the management.

4. Failures were acknowledged publicly — studied for lessons learned and communicated back to employees. Punishment was not tolerated. The Chief Medical Officer modeled the way for all senior leaders by openly acknowledging the failure of his team to bring to launch a blockbuster product that everyone thought was a certainty. He and his direct reports candidly communicated what should have been done versus what was done. An outpouring of support and advice/resources was offered as a result which led to a quicker solution to the problems encountered by the launch team.

5. Senior leadership used every opportunity to advance employee understanding of the strategy, e.g. not just presenting at leadership development classes but teaching in class — getting to know up close and personally the talent in the organization. Leaders teaching current and future leaders builds a strong sense of organizational identity versus outsiders coming in to teach leadership concepts without the experience of the context of the current organization. "Lessons from the Trench's" of these leaders added impact to the training sessions as a result of the context. Participants expressed a deeper understanding of APC's strategic direction, vision, values, and culture.

6. Electronically pulse/survey employees regularly — if you do not know you cannot fix problems or acknowledge successes — small and large. This satisfied the quantitatively focused leaders and employees including the very

powerful CFO and his organization that were critical to securing budget resources for initiatives including leadership development and culture change. Learnings and the changes they surfaced as being needed to successfully execute the strategy were seen as grounded in "reality".

APC's leadership had an unquenchable desire to change the Pharma industry. They also had the same level of desire to know what was going on throughout their organization. They were committed to strategic learning and especially culture change to reach their business goals. Both successes and failures would be openly discussed, reflected on, and actions changed based on their new learnings. As the EC built a global team-based organization, each function was also building their global team-based organization and then forming global teams with other functions. R&D was fully committed to the global strategy, Chapter 5 discusses their experience.

Note: This chapter is based on a case published by John, S. "Transforming the Pharmaceutical Industry: Human Resources as Global Catalyst, Summer 2007". *Organization Development Journal* 25(2) (2007), The Organization Development Institute.

5

Globalizing R&D — The APC Way

Tom had stopped listening to his doctor. Fear and anxiety had taken him over. His doctor saw a glazed eyed frightened patient across his desk. He had read about adult onset diabetes or Type 2 as it is now known. He remembered some very chilling facts about untreated diabetes in adults. Loss of eyesight, amputation of the lower extremities, at worst and at best major changes to diet and lifestyle habits needed to be made. He kept seeing quality of life — poor-going across his closed eyelids. Fear turned to anger and frustration as his physician interrupted his coma-like state.

> *Tom your quality of life would have been great if DD1302, the most innovative treatment to come along in years, was available in sufficient quantities. You see the company that discovered it cannot make enough to meet world wide demand. The World Health Organization (Seidell, 2000) estimates there are 150 million individuals worldwide with diabetes. They also estimate that by 2025, that number will double. This is reaching epidemic proportions. Sorry to say, it may be as long as four years before DD1302 is available to you.*

Not easy news to give to a frightened patient for sure. But let us rewind the video tape on interaction between Tom and his doctor.

Tom, you are in luck. Over the last years a number of innovative therapies have been discovered to help you manage your diabetes and they are available now for your use. The drug companies have been working very hard and smart to help the estimated 150 million adults who presently have Type 2 Diabetes. DD1302 is just such a product. We in the health care community were worried that there wouldn't be enough of DD1302 to meet demand. I don't know how the drug company did it but they did. They took easily two years or more off the normal twelve years it takes to discover a drug and get it to us to prescribe. Innovative drug therapies don't happen often now.

As discussed in Chapter 4, the APC vision and strategy was to create a global team-based organization that was capable of reducing the current 12–15 years from molecule discovery to patient usage to 6–9 years. Achieving this vision would require two things:

1. Global high performing teams (GHPTs) in a function such as R&D, Commercial Operations, or Industrial Operations to be high performing very shortly after formation. These teams within a function would work with disease specialists in a disease area such as diabetes, other disease areas such as cardiology connected to diabetes as well as Information Technology professionals. These in function teams would have the professionals from the above functions, from a number of countries depending upon the therapeutic or disease area.
2. Some members of these in function teams would be selected to work on cross-functional teams where R&D, commercial, and manufacturing personnel were on the team. There would be a cross-functional team for each drug in a disease or therapeutic area.

These teams were expected to work together, respecting their differences, learn together, create new ways of thinking and acting, and finally, transferring their new learnings through knowledge sharing technologies to the overall organization. The global DD1302 team led by R&D, with representatives from the commercial and manufacturing functions, as well as representatives from four key countries — France, Germany, US, and Japan. These countries had a vested interest in bringing sufficient supplies of DD1302 to the patient as quickly as possible. These countries have larger numbers of their population having Type 2 diabetes or a predisposition to getting it. In addition, these countries had capability in the technical areas needed to reduce cycle time from discovery to patient.

Building the Global Team-Based R&D Function

The drug discovery process is a complex and highly risky business. While estimates vary, it is safe to say that of the 10,000 molecules screened for possible drugs safe in humans, only 1 will make it to the patient. Historically, Pharma R&D has operated in a sequential set of phases starting with Discovery and ending with an approved drug. The phases are, in summary, the following:

1. Discovery — Several hundred thousand chemical entities are examined for possible druggable qualities. Druggable means that if a chemical entity were to be approved by a regulatory agency, manufactured, and distributed to patients it would effectively and safely treat the medical condition for which it was approved. Repeated screening leaves approximately 250.

2. Pre-Clinical Testing — The 250 drug candidates are taken forward for testing in animals and the laboratory. It is here that the relationship between drug dosage and toxicity is established. Those drug candidates that are deemed too risky to be useful by humans are dropped.

3. Phase I — Approximately 100 healthy human volunteers are tested for dose toleration without signs of toxicity. For life-threatening diseases such as cancer, the volunteers are ill with the disease being tested for.
4. Phase II Trials — Approximately 100–300 humans are tested to evaluate the safety and efficacy (effectiveness) of the drug candidate. These patients have the disease in question.
5. Phase III — Once the optimal dose and efficacy of the drug candidate is established in Phase II, several thousand patients with the disease are tested for long-term usage and its effects.
6. Phase IV — Successful Phase III studies are then summarized and the data submitted to the FDA (US), EMEA (Europe), and MHW (Japan) for review and approval to market the drug. Once the drug is marketed, Phase IV continues chemical trial studies in large populations to ensure safety and efficacy findings found in Phase III are still valid.

These six phases of drug discovery and distribution have been structured as separate areas within R&D, each having teams work on their responsible area and, then, handing off their work to the next area. This sequential and somewhat siloed work model served the industry well for many decades prior to globalization. A number of innovative drugs were discovered and commercialized this way. An example would be Lipitor, which for over a decade has been helping people lower their blood cholesterol and reduce their chances of getting cardiac disease.

Globalization, as we saw in Part I, has changed the way many businesses and industries conduct research and then develop their products for commercialization. APC, as we discovered, in Chapter 4, was committed to globalizing the entire Pharma value chain.

The Early Days

We must all focus our time and energy on only mission critical initiatives that build competitive advantage. Initiatives spring up everyday in APC. But clearly, we all need to start with the same understanding of our vision, strategy, and priorities. Each of us individually and our teams must make decisions that execute our strategy faster and more effectively than any Pharma company in the world. Our global team organization is the key to future growth.

Chief Medical Officer (CMO), Leadership Forum (2000)

This was a rallying call for the top 200 leaders within APC to put aside functional and regional perspectives and to embrace the global team-based strategy, structure, and culture.

Three core principles would emerge from the top 200 Leadership Forum that year. These core principles would act as the foundation for deploying the needed initiatives to successfully operationalize APC's vision and strategy. The core principles were:

1. Move from siloed teams and sequential discovery to patient phases to global teams looking at these phases in parallel when possible. This would dramatically reduce the hand off from team to team since a core group would be on the team throughout the phases.
2. Leverage the rich diversity of expertise, experience, and thought leadership to stimulate innovation and action that would drive out waste and inefficiency. Utilize strategic learning (SL) techniques to focus the learning from successes and failures.
3. Transfer the team-created knowledge across the organization for all to benefit. Lead the necessary change to the organizations strategy, structure, operations, and/or culture.

All three core principles would need to be working to achieve the APC vision of bringing high-value drugs to patients across the world in 9 years or less. Tom, our recently diagnosed Type 2 diabetic, would be a grateful recipient of the leadership of APC both in R&D and across the commercial and manufacturing functions. Successfully utilizing SL and leading change principles would ensure that the global team-based organization takes root and flourishes within APC. DD1302 would be one drug that the new paradigm would be applied to. Before discussing how Tom and many others would benefit from the APC strategy, we turn to how the APC R&D addressed the CMO's concern of everyone being on the same page regarding their understanding and alignment to the strategy.

Enabling Strategy Execution

The APC R&D strategy was to build and sustain a high-performing culture. As discussed earlier, the measure of high performance was bringing new molecules to the patient between 6 and 9 years. In addition, could existing products' performance be improved by using the R&D strategy tools? The R&D Leadership Team (RDLT) was committed to these strategic priorities. They would be easily measured since each year the CMO presented to financial analysts worldwide how effectively R&D delivered on potential products in the pipeline as well as how existing products were improved to yield additional financial results.

The RDLT defined their High-Performance Culture with three components:

1. Great company brand/culture — a values driven and focused well-communicated strategy.
2. Great work/jobs — jobs that connected and aligned directly to the strategy.
3. Great performance/rewards/development systems — exceptional individual and team performance was recognized and rewarded. Potential was identified in the Talent

Management Reviews and were offered accelerated development opportunities.

The RDLT with the EC finalized the upcoming year's strategic priorities by late November. These priorities clearly spelled out the goals and deliverables at the overall global organization level, global function level, and the cross-function level. By early December, the goals/deliverables were cascaded throughout APC. The RDLT worked with their direct reports to translate their goals/deliverables into the goals/deliverables for their direct reports. This process was repeated until all levels of the organization had been briefed on the strategic priorities, goals, and deliverables and the resources available to achieve their goals/deliverables.

The RDLT, in collaboration with the Commercial and Industrial functions, developed a tool set that enabled their employees and teams to rapidly become high performing. The RDLT looked to global and functional HR to facilitate the use of these tools, as well as acting as the lead culture change agents. The RDLT developed in early 2000 that the quality of leadership in all functions would have to be improved if they were to succeed in executing their strategy. Chapter 6 discusses building global leadership capability and Chapter 7 discusses the role of HR.

The tool set developed and deployed first in R&D and later throughout the APC organization was as follows:

1. One Page Strategy — each hierarchal level of the organization starting at the global function level would develop a one page strategy document to use as a cascading tool for the next level below.
2. GHPTs were formed around a product. The teams included personnel from R&D, commercial, industrial, and support functions such as HR, legal, communications, IT, and Strategic Alliances/Partnerships (external).
3. A SL process that would facilitate quickly learning from experiences and provide a template for change.

4. Knowledge Sharing Process/Systems to transfer the team-created knowledge to the larger organization.

Each tool is discussed below, however, taken together these tools provided APC as well as the global functions with a systemic way to move from strategic priorities to execution to learning from success and failures to revising strategic priorities and repeating the process to achieve their goal of reducing cycle time from molecule discovery to patient by 50 percent.

The One Page Strategy

The year 2000 was a good year for APC. The financial analysts were very positive about how effectively APC had integrated the two companies and were visibly making progress in building their global team-based organization. The APC leadership — The EC — was driven to succeed for sure. Just as important as succeeding, was doing so quickly. A sense of urgency became their mantra along with the networked organization where global teams executed the strategy and shared their learnings. In reviewing their year 1 performance, their perspective and feedback from "pulses" taken across the organization there were indications that many employees/teams saw the strategy as complex and complicated. If 2001 was to be a great year, this would have to be fixed quickly.

The One Page Strategy emerged from the RDLT deliberations. This One Page had two key goals:

1. Bringing 2–3 high potential new molecules to approval each year.
2. Increase productivity across the pipeline value chain (Discovery, Phase I, II, III, and IV) and reduce cycle time to 6–9 years.

Each of these goal areas had activities and measurable contributions (deliverables) directly under them. An example for the point 2 above would be to develop people to work on GHPTs and to support the network-centric culture of APC.

The RDLT prepared their One Page Strategy, which was at the global function level. Each of the four major countries then prepared their One Page Strategy. Similarly each area of the pipeline prepared a One Page Strategy (Discovery, Pre-clinical, Phase I, Phase II, Phase III, and Phase IV). Finally HR, IS, and Knowledge Management (KM) prepared One Page Strategies as well. Individuals and teams would then set goals aligned to their respective One Page Strategy. KM was part of the R&D HR function. It was the responsibility of HR and KM specifically to work with teams to prepare their One Page Strategy and goals/activities to support their work.

The RDLT, Country Heads, Heads of Functional areas as well as employees could easily see the cascading of strategic priorities, goals, activities, and contributions for their areas as well as the other areas of the organization. Gaps could more easily be seen in advance rather than as lessons learned from failures. These One Page Strategies became the operating charter of each of the GHPT which is discussed next.

Global High-Performing Teams

The news could not have been better. A new drug submission to the FDA was approved. This success was sweet after a bitter failure of the team to obtain the approval a year earlier. This was an important new drug that was needed in the fight against infections causing pneumonia, bronchitis, and sinusitis. The CMO noted:

> *I salute the team for their rapid recovery from the earlier failure. Failure can be a devastating experience if you let it be. This team wouldn't give up — they sought outside coaches and mentors to identify what went wrong (in the team process) and fixed it — fast.*

In analyzing the team's performance, four lessons emerged:

1. Roles were confused and ambiguous in the failed team. The same team regrouped themselves, clarified their roles, and supported each other in the discipline of staying in role once innovation gave way to the process of filing the Approval Registration.
2. An unprecedented amount of data had been collected during the clinical trials. This enormous data set caused confusion and added to role clarity. The successful team was able to sort out data points from anecdotal support for the product from patients.
3. Cross-functional expertise was critical. Scientific, marketing, manufacturing, and information technology expertise all needed to be identified and then synthesized into an understandable and compelling filing.
4. Tireless execution, scientific rigor, functions (non-scientific) supplying expertise, and best solutions as well as successful utilization of internal and external networks and thought leaders.

The FDA complimented the APC team on bringing forward an innovative first in class product to patients. The GHPT concept worked — not the first time out but it worked in bringing a new product to market.

The RDLT, utilizing the knowledge sharing process to be discussed later, insisted that all GHPTs analyze their performance and identify lessons learned to be transferred to larger organization. As a result, five best practices were codified for all teams to check for as they went through the team life cycle. These five best practices were:

1. There needs to be a true partnership amongst the three partners. The three partners are: senior leadership, team leader, and team members. There are clear expectations of each partner as well as their contribution to the tasks

the team must perform as well as the way they treat each other (maintenance).

2. High performing (HP) teams know when to address tasks or relationships to their advantage. This capability enables the team to reach its goals quicker than non-high performing teams. Speaking up to facilitate high performance is characteristic of these teams whether it is the senior leader, team leader, or team member.

3. HP teams demonstrate a high level of proficiency in goal setting. Their goals are aligned to strategy and they flex and change goals as the strategy emerges/evolves. They appear to do this effortlessly with little disagreement or rancor exhibited.

4. The processes they use are meant to be efficient and effective. Their team reaches high-performance levels without wasting time.

5. These teams are successful at codifying their learning, creating new ways of looking at business situations and delivering solutions on time, at quality, at or below cost. They utilize their partnership trust with senior leadership to transfer these learnings/team-created knowledge to the overall organization.

These learnings were captured over the 2000–2002 time-frame. They would become important to developing a global business leader curriculum that would produce leaders at all levels of the organization. The HR/KM Consulting Group, after extensive work with the GHPT, developed a SL frame-work that could be utilized to clarify the changes needed and assisted teams in preparing the organization for needed change.

Strategic Learning in R&D

DD1302 was already in production and was in short supply. Each country was allocated a percentage of what the demand was for that country. DD1302 had gone through the discovery to product launch phases in the historical pattern of sequential phases with a separate (siloed) team for each phase handing off its work to the next phase's team. By the time DD1302 got to the sales forecasting team and the manufacturing team, it was too late to build additional plant capacity to meet patient demand. Tom, our diabetes patient, would most likely have to wait as long as 4 years. APC R&D made the decision to apply the GHPT concept to reduce the 48 months to 36 months or less if at all possible.

The cross-functional/regional team formed quickly to define the problem and develop solutions. They called upon internal HR/KM Consultants and when needed external resources were identified to help guide them in their work. A SL loop that resulted in an innovative solution to the supply problem was needed. The team went to work. They devised a question and answer (Q&A) focused approach to solving the supply/plant capacity problem. They developed the following Q & A process:

1. What product problem or innovation do we need? Ask why 5 times.
2. What modifications to process or assets can we envision? Blue Sky.
3. What must be done to process or assets to have #2 happen?
4. What did we plan to do?
5. What did we do?
6. Why is there a gap? What must be done to successfully execute?
7. What did we learn? Do same, change/modify, stop doing?

These straightforward questions brought the team together very quickly. Solutions were generated; scenario-planning techniques were utilized to eliminate options. Their best thinking produced a plan that when executed expanded plant capacity to meet patient demand from 48 months to approximately 36 months. Other GHPTs started to adopt the SL process the DD1302 team pioneered.

Step number 7, summarizing the learning brings us to the area the RDLT had the most apprehension about bringing to the EC for possible changes to the strategy, structure, operations, or culture. They were asking diverse people — technical expertise, generational, nationalities, gender, race, etc. — to openly share what they had learned to reduce the learning curve of other teams. This would require a trust level of senior management that is rare in today's environment. The individuals and teams that openly shared their newly created knowledge would have to trust management that they would be recognized for their larger contribution to the execution of the APC global strategy. The EC would have to show by its actions that it could fairly and credibly evaluate people's individual and team performance and recognize/reward appropriately. But first the knowledge sharing had to take place before the EC could be tested to do the right thing.

Knowledge Sharing in R&D

The HR/KM team was committed to working with GHPTs to promote connectivity between people on a team, between teams, and with the overall organization. Their goal was to simplify the creation, sharing, and use of knowledge to give APC a competitive advantage. The ultimate measure of success would be the reduction in cycle time to bring new and innovative therapies to patients. In addition, problems such as DD1302 would have measurable improvements from using GHPTs as well as KM tools. KM in APC and especially in R&D was seen as both a strategy, i.e. a conscious selection of the value of KM concepts and a KM set of tools and procedures. KM as a strategy and tool set would enable R&D to share their learnings and changes within their function as well as with the other functions.

The HR/KM team offered a variety of services. Their primary responsibility was in working with GHPTs to produce their One Page Strategy. They also utilized the SL process to identify

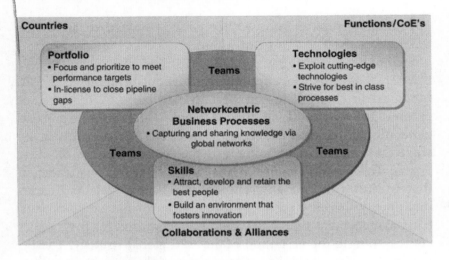

FIGURE 5.1 HR/KM SL Areas.

and solve problems and to stimulate innovation. They worked with existing GHPTs as well as start-ups. Figure 5.1 shows a partial listing of their offerings.

HR/KM also led the formation of a number of communities of practices. Communities were formed around the major processes of the Discovery to Launch value chain. For example, a global community was formed around supply chain, i.e. the manufacturing function needs to produce the drug. Communities were also formed around the Regulatory Process to help streamline and speed up the filing of Approval Applications in the US, France, Germany, and Japan. Figure 5.2 describes the benefits of communities.

To further the goals of building and sustaining a network-centric organization, the RDLT supported these additional KM tools:

1. K-mail — knowledge expertise locator through e-mail.
2. Lessons learned through stories — text, audio, video site for placing lessons learned for others to see and utilize.
3. Champions of Knowledge Sharing — internal recognition of knowledge sharing by senior leadership. Communicated

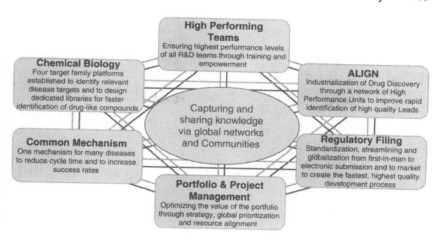

FIGURE 5.2 Increasing Productivity through Communities of Practice.

to the entire company at Global Town Hall Meetings and posted on the organization's senior leadership intranet site.

APC R&D had accomplished a lot in the 3 years since the integration. Much more needs to be done. There were still lingering cultural integration issues to work through. Employee surveys over those years clearly showed that APC needed to significantly improve its leadership capability to form and successfully lead GHPTs. HR also needed to significantly improve its capability to work with these teams. Chapter 6 discusses the challenges of developing global leaders and Chapter 7 discusses the new role of HR and how it prepared itself to deliver on the organization's expectations.

Reference

Seidell, J. C. "Obesity, Insulin Resistance, and Diabetes — A Worldwide Epidemic." *British Journal of Nutrition* 83(Suppl 1), S5–S8.

6

Building Global Leadership Capability

If we are to succeed now and into the future, we must field the best global team's in our industry. It is critical we invest in our management team who will boldly lead us into the future.

CEO APC January (2001)

APC had a good year in 2000, the first full year operating as an integrated company. However, good was not good enough for the senior leadership team. The top 200 met in late January of 2001 to identify and agree on both the enablers and the impediments to executing their strategy. Unanimously, they agreed that the global team based organization (GHPT) strategy was the strategy of choice. If successful, they would revolutionize the Pharma industry model. Tom, our diabetes friend, as well as millions of others, would be major beneficiaries of their success. The therapeutic areas of oncology, metabolism, cardiology, and central nervous system (Alzheimer's) would all see major time savings in bringing life saving drugs to the patient.

The top 200 conference participants had analyzed their global high performing teams (GHPTs) performance and had submitted detailed recommendations. Recommendations, that for successful teams like DD1302, would move future teams to even higher levels of performance. They also, courageously, provided recommendations for less successful teams as well as failed teams. There were no efforts to mask the identities of teams — successful or failed or in-between. As one participant noted, "There is no place to hide in this organization. Learn from your experience and change quickly or perish".

APC was a place to flourish if you and your team were willing to learn as the strategy was being executed and, then, willing to change (sometimes radically) based upon your team's learning. More difficult was learning from other team's learning's/changes and to be willing to take the risk of changing from other's experience. For many, quite an unsettling proposition. As a result, there was some voluntary turnover in APC early on. The way APC was moving was not for everyone. Exit interview data showed most people left to go to Pharma companies that were still operating with the siloed team approach to drug development.

There was unanimous agreement amongst the Top 200 as the conference ended. The GHPT strategy was on target but execution capability needed to be ramped up significantly. Building global team leadership capability would be the primary focus of 2001 and 2002. Success, here, would be critical if APC was to meet its stated business goals. Everyone was watching — employees, competitors, financial analysts, governmental regulatory agencies, industry thought leaders, and patients and physicians. Chapter 4 discussed about the ALTs formed in 2000 to tackle organizational strategy, structure, and culture. These ALTs were designed with Just in Time Leadership development provided by their facilitator (usually an HR Professional), i.e. in team Leadership development. The Top 200, still supportive of the ALT model, agreed that this type of in team leadership development would not be enough in the days ahead. Dedicated development experiences at the global organization level would be needed and needed quickly. GHR was asked to take the lead in making their recommendations a reality. Time was of the essence — urgent action was required.

APC had experienced a great deal of success with the ALT approach in 2000. The EC decided with the Head of GHR to move ahead, in 2001, with this approach. The goal was to build global business leaders, at all levels and locations, of the organization in large numbers between 2001 and 2003.

The Global Leadership Development Task Force (GLDT)

GHR went immediately to work. Before the Top 200 conference participants left, task force members were identified and committed to a one-week Leadership Capability meeting before the end of the third quarter, 2001. In addition, a globally led HR team was formed and ready to meet and set-up the project plan within one week of the end of the Top 200 Conference.

The GHR strategy for the GLDT was straightforward. A one-week offsite would be designed and held before the end of third quarter. Approximately 40–45 Senior Business Leaders would be invited. These business leaders would have representatives from the EC, the 12 key countries, and the global functions — commercial, manufacturing, R&D, and support functions (Legal, HR, Corporate Alliances, Communications, and Information Systems). The CEO would kick-off "the task force meeting", followed by the GHR. In addition, an external thought leader would be selected to set the stage for building an effective leadership pipeline for the APC GHPT strategy.

The EC was expecting GHR to provide solutions as outputs of the GLDT meeting. The goals that emerged out of the Top 200 Conference were:

1. Formulate a strategy for developing global leaders across all levels/regions.
2. Identify the capabilities needed for these global leaders — confirm or modify the APC Leadership Profile (ALP) that had been developed in early 2000.
3. Recommend how goals 1 and 2 could be quickly developed.
4. Design a global Talent Management process that would enable senior leadership to identify high-potential talent, i.e. those who could most quickly develop global team leadership capabilities.

In less than six months, the GHR team had to collect data on the four goals, benchmark best practices in/out of the industry, design the one-week GLDT meeting, and set-up a process for the EC to review the results of these efforts and to find immediate deployment — all while HR was meeting existing work loads in supporting GHPT and HR core deliverables such as On-Boarding, Supervisory Skills Development, compensation and benefits, and performance management systems.

The GHR team, in parallel to the above responsibility areas, would reach out to academic institutions, global consulting firms, thought leaders, and other providers of global leadership education. The APC business strategy was set and would only receive minor "tweaks" over 2001 and 2002. This provided some stability in planning what content leadership programs might contain as well as what job assignments, task forces, etc., would be made available to participants. Confirming and/or modifying the ALP would have to wait until the GLDT meeting was completed and summarized for the EC. Specific capabilities and in what form they would be developed could then be built into leadership programs or the Talent Management (TM) process. In this way, the first leadership programs/task forces, etc., could be deployed in 2001.

Our overarching goal was to identify the capabilities that three levels of management or leadership would need to move APC into a globally recognized pharmaceutical company. The three levels were:

1. Supervisors;
2. Managers of managers; and
3. Senior level-officer level (VP) to CEO.

Our process for identifying the leadership capabilities for the above categories was:

- Identify from the talent management system those senior leaders that modeled global leadership capability — these leaders represented functions such as R&D, sales and marketing, industrial operations, and support functions from all regions, e.g. the Americas, Europe, Asia, Middle East and Africa.
- There would be three teams. Team one would identify what supervisors would need to become global leaders.

Team two would identify what managers of managers would need and team three would identify the same for senior leaders-officers to CEO. Core capabilities, such as what every leader in APC would need would be surfaced and defined.

- Each team would have a leader from the business units identified in step one. Each team would have one HR department member as a facilitator to keep discussions on track.

- Our CEO, global head of HR and a distinguished thought leader from the academic world, Ram Charan, a Harvard professor who has written books on leadership, building the leadership pipeline, would start the week. Each team would work separately during the day with a general session at days' end to share progress and insights. As an aside, web-based technology was used for voting in the general sessions and to share summaries, learnings and progress from each of the teams.

- During the week, senior leaders from APC would visit, sharing their perspectives on challenges facing APC and the industry itself.

- By the end of the week, each team's output would be discussed, reconciled, and core capabilities across all levels of leaders would be agreed on. Ways of developing each level's capability would also be discussed. It was agreed that the Global Org Effectiveness/Executive Education Department would ultimately decide on the methods for developing capability.

- Within 30 days from adjourning we would summarize our work and recommendations to the CEO and send the recommendations to a sub-team from the GLDT meeting to review and approve.

- Within 60 days of the group's feedback, our team would prepare a report and present it to the CEO and his team for approval.

We asked the GLDT participants to come prepared to discuss and confirm or modify the existing ALP that we provided below:

Deliver Strategic Business Results

Focuses on Customer and Market Value Creation

Establishes a Compelling Vision with Clearly Focused Priorities

Drives for Speed in Decisions and Actions

Integrates and Balances Global and Local Perspectives

Demonstrate Personal Leadership

Delivers on Commitments

Engages Others through Active and Visible Communication

Demonstrates Adaptability, Flexibility and Resourcefulness

Leads Courageously

Build the Global Organization

Adapts and Leverages Technology and Best Practices

Fosters Connectivity and Collaboration Across the Organization

Builds Flexible and Productive Alliances

Capitalizes on Multicultural, Diverse Organizational Strengths

Develop Human Capital

Attracts and Retains the Best Talent and Team

Empowers and Enables Others to Act

Maintains High and Fair Accountability for Actions and Results

Provides Constructive Feedback and Coaching

Transform and Relevant the Business

Challenges the Status Quo

Identifies and Pursues New, Untapped ideas and Opportunities

Continually Raises the Organization's Level of Ambition

Anticipates, Creates and Embraces Change.

The first order of business was to confirm the ALP. After some lively discussions in the large group of 45 senior leaders followed by small team discussion, the ALP was confirmed as the going forward Leadership Profile for APC. The GLDT worked diligently over the week to accomplish the goals set by the EC. Each of the three teams was structured as a mirror to the GHPTs used to execute the APC strategy. After the first morning kick-off by the CEO, the GHR, and Ram Charan, the teams met to discuss their individual charter, returning at days end to share their learnings with the larger group. This process was repeated each morning and afternoon throughout the week. Areas of disagreement were openly discussed and resolved by week's end. A set of guiding principles emerged:

1. Leaders act as teachers to their teams.
2. Leaders coach individuals and teams for high performance.
3. We work with best in — class academic institutions and consulting firms as partners.
4. The GHPTs strategy is our core capability area to develop in all leaders, managers, and individual contributors.
5. Everyone and all teams are expected to transfer lessons learned to the larger organization whether in success or failure.
6. A sense of urgency is critical to our success and our culture must support it.

More detailed capabilities also emerged from the week:

1. The ability to set stretch goals directly aligned to the GHPT strategy is important for all leader/manager levels.
2. Knowing how to utilize strategic learning techniques and tools to deliver team results is a core capability.
3. Being able to identify the enablers and impediments to strategy execution and then structuring and leading necessary change.

All three teams noted the importance of being in touch with the social networks (informal and formal) that exist and being able to utilize these networks to accomplish needed change.

GHR summarized the deliverables that surfaced at week's end:

1. Talent Management must be revamped immediately to identify high-potential current and future leaders beyond the Top 200 and provide structured leadership development experiences and challenging work assignments to accelerate their growth.
2. A Leadership Education Curriculum (LEC) must be designed for rollout by early 2002. Three programs were specified — one for senior leaders (all officers), second for manager of managers (GHPT leaders), and third a computer-based simulation for all supervisors/managers to keep the leadership pipeline full. A program would be offered that teaches people how to coach for high performance.

The GHR team was ready to proceed immediately thanks to the parallel processing work they did over spring and summer. GHR was the lead, however, R&D HR/KM stepped up to assume major responsibilities in designing and deploying both Talent Management changes and the LEC.

It was a very productive week. Everyone left excited and engaged — ready to work. As the team leader that worked on what Senior Leader's capabilities needed to be developed said:

APC leaders are the soul of APC. Those leaders leverage our strengths into a global organization ... Courageous and ambitious leadership is key to our successfully executing our Global Team Based strategy.

When implemented, these changes would produce profound effects on the APC culture. One major change that kept surfacing during the week was the leader as teacher role.

Tichy (2004) speaks directly to the power of this principle being put into action "… building a teaching organization is not about being soft or fuzzy. It is about building high-performing teams of leader/teachers". He goes on to quote David Novak of PepsiCo, "There is no way that we could have grown this business so fast and prepared it for the future [without leaders teaching leaders]".

Nobody could have predicted what happened next. With senior support, we thought that implementation of the workgroup's recommendations was certain; we could not have been more wrong. In autumn 2001, we brought our recommendations to the CEO. He approved building a full curriculum for the three levels of leadership described earlier. We would use the APC leadership profile as the starting point for creating the courses for each level. We would contract with either world-class academic business schools, such as Harvard, London School of Business or INSEAD, or with internationally known consulting firms, such as Mercer Delta or Deloitte Touche to finalize our Leadership Development strategy and implement the programs. It was expected that we would offer the curriculum to our line leaders by the second quarter of 2002.

The CEO's retreat was held in November 2001 and included all his direct reports, one of whom was the global head of HR. He would represent the suggested curriculum and the implementation plan and budget for 2002/03. The retreat participants endorsed the presentation in full. That was it, we were up and running. We received the go-ahead on a Wednesday evening and started calling universities and consulting firms for proposals. On Friday, at the close of the retreat, budgets were discussed and confirmed. Our budget was cut, not by a little, but completely. The reasons given were that there was not enough short-term payback. We received the call on Friday night. The EC had elected to continue sponsoring initiatives that were currently producing strategic learning and the appropriate changes to strategy, structure, operations, and/ or the culture.

It would be October 2002, almost a year later, before the approval and budget came. And it was only a partial victory as we were to start the global leadership development with our managers of managers. We would defer development experiences for senior leaders and supervisors indefinitely. The EC would still be holding this group accountable for identifying strategic learnings and transferring them to the overall organization as well as leading culture change through the social networks that had been created during the early integration efforts of APC as well as the new networks that were created as the global team strategy was being executed.

The managers-of-managers group was seen as critical change agents in globalizing APC. This group could influence their direct reports, peers, and senior leaders they reported to. These were upper-level middle managers who had significant specialized technical knowledge in their disciplines. They were high-performing sales and marketing, R&D, and industrial operations professionals. Others were support professionals in law, HR, communications, finance, or alliances.

The Talent Management process had matured in the merged organization and was identifying high-potential future leaders who would need and demand world-class development experiences in their work assignments and in executive programs.

Good fortune smiled on us. As discussed in Chapter 4, in May 2002, a new head of global HR took over. He was a line executive, head of one of our major countries and became a member of the management board. He was briefed and quickly understood the needs of our future leaders and how our recommendations were supportive of these needs. He presented our recommendations to the chairman and in October 2002 we started to build the first global business leader program that had been postponed by the EC at the CEO's Retreat in 2001.

In the mean time, we utilized the GHR team strategy of parallel processing consulting firms. We had identified a firm that would develop, for our supervisors and managers, a computer-based simulation customized to reflect our Global Team-Based Organization strategy. We proceeded to build this simulation in the summer of 2001. We piloted the program in 2002 and then secured approval and funding to roll it out throughout the organization. We also, simultaneously, identified the academic institutions we would work with to design and deliver the global Manager-of-Manager programs. Our senior leaders would teach in the supervisors and manager-of-manager programs. In addition, we contracted with IMD in Lausanne for their Learning Network program. This program provides 30 min Thought Leader web casts with a different topic every week. These voluntary web casts are available for seven days until the next topic is released. In this way all three populations, i.e. Manager of Managers, supervisors/managers, and employees would have an opportunity to be exposed to strategic learning and leading change concepts.

Building Global Leadership Education

We decided quickly on a US-based business school and a European one to work together to provide a unique experience for our leaders. The program would take place over three weeks in total. Week one in the US, week two would take place in Europe about three months later, and the program's third week would be held approximately one year after week two. The participants would come from all over the world, representing all our function areas. They would be selected from the Talent Management process and must be a future leader or demonstrate high potential to qualify and be a manager of managers.

Each group would master topics such as strategy execution, working across functions, and most importantly working across cultures. In addition, personal leadership development would be emphasized. Leading change, and building and sustaining global networks were critical skills that needed to be developed by this group. Each topic area was designed to have a brief lecturette on the theory of the topic with best practice examples from industry provided, case studies/role plays, small team exercises, and simulations if available for that topic. The small teams formed during week one were to stay networked until week two and to exchange strategic learnings they were utilizing with their part of the organization and the changes being implemented as a result of their learnings.

We scheduled six groups for 2003, approximately 300 participants at 50 per group. Global terrorism and war in Iraq sent chills through APC. Travel was restricted to essential only. We held our breath as the management board pondered cancelling the first group in April 2003. The chairman deemed the program essential business travel — we were on our way.

Our first group concluded week two in June 2003. Our closing module on Friday asked teams to come back with action plans. No surprises: listen better, communicate more often, delegate better, and so on. They left each other to their individual action plans and wished each other well until they met again the following June for the third week. R&D participants, however, committed to integrating their learnings into their KM tool set described in Chapter 5.

The second group started in October 2003 in the US with their second week in Europe in January 2004. The program had been revised and was gaining a strong reputation within the organization. APC executives, including management board members were teaching in the classroom. There was a lot to learn and great networking with peers and APC executives beyond the classroom. In addition to APC executives teaching in the classroom, other APC executives came to the session in the evening for dinner and drinks. They shared their views on the APC global strategy, learnings to date, and how the participants might further contribute to the strategy execution efforts. These fireside chats as they became to be known were always rated by the participants as a major source of learning and how to apply it back in their part of the organization.

Group two had a magical quality about it. You could sense it from the first week. They were special; they were connected and acted like a community from the start. On the Friday afternoon of the second week the teams presented their action plans. Thirty minutes before we were adjourning, a participant raised his hand and asked for some time at the front of the room. He rose out of his seat and came to the front of the amphitheatre. No one knew what to expect and what happened next took everyone by surprise. He stuttered and then spat it out. The group wanted to form a community, a global community of change agents. Their purpose was to payback APC for investing in them and believing in their leadership potential.

They presented a simple concept — parts of APC that needed change advice but could not afford expensive outside consultants could come to the change agent community on the APC Intranet (formed by group two), and post their problems. Individuals from the group would volunteer and have contact with the APC function unit needing the service or advice. A small team of change agents from group two would be formed if needed, depending on the complexity of the situation. They would utilize the tools, processes, and concepts they had learned in weeks one and two as the foundations for their services. Once again, R&D with their KM Network of Communities, discussed in Chapter 5, advanced strategic learning and leading change. They had moved beyond the R&D function to organizational level strategic learning and change leadership.

They discussed the community to be formed for 30 min. They talked of their vision, purpose, and structure, and how they would get this started. Their spirits rose and fell. At the end, they agreed to move forward, one participant would set-up the e-room platform. The date was 11 January. Time would tell. A month went by and no action had been taken. By 17 February there was a breakthrough. The e-room developer emailed me for group two's participant list, the e-room is ready to deploy. By the end of the month the virtual room is up and running. Community is part of the culture here at APC and R&D was taking a global leadership role in forming a very powerful way for people to transfer strategic learning and leading change throughout the organization.

What Group Two Did

Senior management had requested that business leaders focus on their functions and countries. John (2004) noted several things that emerged from group two during this period of approximately five months:

- Sub-networks formed around functions. Participants from all locations were connecting and encouraged to share information about how they were applying the leadership skills learned during weeks one and two of the program.
- Several participants who led the formation of the change agent community at the end of week two in January stayed connected. They shared the successes and failures of their peers who acted as change agents but did not always post their efforts in the e-room. This led to the lessons learned in the sub-networks being distributed across the larger group of participants.
- Individual change agents surfaced from group two that, because of local circumstances related more to their function and region, required them to step up quickly and make themselves more visible in their part of the organization.
- Work teams were under a great deal of pressure to deliver top-notch results to their senior leaders. At the same time, these work teams were aware that they were being acquired and would lose their jobs as a result of the take-over.
- Directors and senior directors were visibly leading the defense and business-as-usual strategy — group two

members or participants were beginning to surface as effective change leaders.

APC was acquired in the summer of 2004. As a result, the building of a cadre of global business leaders was put on hold. The new integrated company would determine what skills their business leaders would need, when they would develop these skills and who would receive this development. It would be early 2005 before all this was finalized. Group two members or participants, however, refused to stop practicing the change skills they had learned and were committed to using in the organization.

Group two had identified a number of IT professionals from various functions and countries. Their sub-network kicked into high gear. They connected virtually, formed a technology plan and, most importantly, a change plan, for consideration by the integration-team leaders. They asked each local technology professional to reach out to their counterpoint in the acquiring company and start discussions about strategy, process, and implementation of merged systems. The group two change agents then connected the sub-networks into a single network that supported both companies. Day one saw employees of both companies able to connect via e-mail, voice mail, and the intranet.

Group two change agents had this to say: "Thanks to the leadership-development experience and my network from the session, the impact of integration across functions and countries was quickly understood. We used the change tools and communities from R&D that we were taught; drafted a strategy and implementation plan; took the lead and the risk — fought the nay sayers and led a cross-organization team to integrate the systems architecture on time, at high quality, and at low cost. We now have a much larger network of IT professionals in the new company".

APC R&D distinguished itself in applying the strategic learning and leading change concepts they learned at their leadership development program. They inspired and supported their colleagues, e.g. IT to take on change leadership roles informed by strategic lessons learned. The new organization has a different view of the Pharma world. In any case, everyone benefits when an individual, team, function improves the workplace, and so do the patients like Tom. Chapter 7 discusses how R&D led the APC culture change from 2000 to their acquisition in 2004.

References

John, S. "Business transformation through leadership development." *Knowledge Management, Ark Group* 7 (8) (2004).
Tichy, N. M. *The Cycle of Leadership: How Great Leaders Teach their Companies to Win*. New York: HarperCollins, 2004.

7

R&D Leads the APC Culture Change

The floor below the catwalk was noisy and bustling with people moving randomly from workstation to workstation. These workstations from SUN were sophisticated pieces of high technology for sure. All the members hovered around the workstation monitor for awhile and then moved on. There did not seem to be a permanent team anywhere on the floor. At the end of the room, above their heads, were two separate large electronic display monitors — black backgrounds with one display having green electronic print and the other display that off orange color. The display on the left had financial news continuously running. The right display had general stories continuously running. The city was Chicago; the news on both displays covered the world. The year 1994 and derivatives were the hottest financial instruments that hungry investors, corporations, and institutional buyers (pension funds) were buying.

These nomads on the floor were creating the next hottest derivative. They worked feverishly, collaborating for a while and, then, moving on to a different workstation to see what was going on there — could they add value to the team at that station? They were competitive with each other and collegial all at the same time. These were graduates (top of their class) from some of the most prestigious academic institutions in the world. People with math, science, and business degrees, as well as heavy interest in technology, worked effortlessly together. Serious, then laughing, and at times talking over each other, they knew their competitors in other similar labs in other cities around the world were trying to beat them to the marketplace. You had to be comfortable with complexity, ambiguity, and paradox. You had to be comfortable knowing that the sales function would only have 21 days to maximize derivative sales before the competition improved on your product. The cycle of creation, release to sales, and innovating in less than three weeks was exhilarating. This was a global product for a 24/7 world.

The Managing Director (MD), responsible for recruiting and development of these high-skilled professionals, described the culture as "in time". Each worker was in the moment looking at the dual display boards to make sense of the current state of the world and connecting to the derivative creation process on the workstation screen.

One floor below, the Business Process Reengineering (BPR) teams were approaching their work quite differently. They were working on documenting the functions present processes and outputs including intended hand-offs between work units in a function and subsequent hand-offs across functions. One team was charged with documenting the Derivative Creation process and hand-offs to risk management and sales. The same MD, also responsible for recruiting and developing the BPR group, described their culture as "through time". The nature of their work required them to make sense of the present process and to create innovative process changes well into the future. How the financial world might change and what must be changed internally to meet these changes was their challenge.

As the financial services world globalized, the senior leadership had its hands full developing a strategy, operations, and culture that could accommodate both sub-cultures. High performance in the current period was required if the organization was to be an attractive investment for share-holders, a magnet drawing the smartest financial people in the world to work there, and to have customers eager for their products and services. The senior leadership also needed to be preparing for the future, uncertain as it might be, to sustain the organization over the long term.

These challenges are not unlike the ones APC faced in 2000 as it formulated its strategy, operations, and culture. As the financial services world was globalizing and adjusting to these challenges, the strategic learning and leading culture change lessons were also applicable to the Pharma world. The sales and manufacturing functions were much like the derivatives creation function, i.e. an "in time" culture albeit longer than 21 days. R&D was much more like BPR, i.e. a "through time" culture that lasted a decade or longer for the R&D leadership team and for people working in one of the phases described in Chapter 5, the time period was in years. A senior leadership challenge if there ever was one. Time is but one element of culture that must be understood and managed.

The Hay Group (2002) emphasizes different characteristics of culture than time discussed above that senior leadership must understand and provide for to execute strategy. Hay tells a story about a medical supply multinational company that shares many of the strategic challenges that APC R&D faced. The supply company was committed to a strategy that significantly reduced product design to customer usage cycle time, that focused on high-profit customer needs, and that delivered innovative products to their customers.

The Senior Team, according to Hay Group, did all the right things. The goals were clear and communicated to all employees. Performance Management processes and systems were in place for employees to set their goals, deliver results, and get evaluated/rewarded based on performance. Cross-functional goals — product design, sales, and manufacturing — were set in the Performance Management system. The senior leadership team, that formulated the strategy, was committed to executing it. All seemed right in their world; the CEO was certain everyone "got it". Execution would be a slam dunk.

The CEO did a "walk around" four months after the plan was set into motion. He was horrified at what he found. New

Product Design had reduced cycle time but had not taken into account increased cycle time manufacturing would need to produce the product. Net result so far, cycle time increased over the old product design. Sales refused to change their work habits of selling to high-volume buyers. Profit margins are low here. They apparently made no efforts to prospect for high-margin buyers and build relationships to sell to them over the longer term. To the CEO's horror even his management team was not sticking to the new direction. The very people who created the new strategy!

Hay Group presents a compelling case that setting clear goals, accountabilities, roles, and even with clear/focused communications is not sufficient for execution success. They suggest that a "culture of dialogue" coupled with a strong Performance Management/rewards program is a winning combination. People stayed in their silos. A shared understanding of what needed to be learned and done differently was not achieved in the first four months.

People open up silos, not Corporate Directives and changes in policy. People need to get to know each other — their world view, mind-sets, beliefs, and values. People need to feel comfortable with each other's skills that will be brought to bear in executing the new strategic direction. Goal clarity, through dialogue, is critical and starts the strategy execution process in the right direction. Leadership keeps execution on track. Culture supports people as they execute and, more importantly, empowers them to change activities as needed on the ground as execution is occurring. A shared culture empowers people to speak up as a new strategic direction emerges and not just follow policy blindly. The military and Olympic teams provide working models for business enterprises to learn from in this area.

Special Operations teams (Seals, Green Berets, and Delta Force), Top Gun Pilot teams, and Olympic teams such as hockey are trained to spend the time necessary upfront building a deep shared understanding of the strategy, goals, and activities needed by everyone on the team to execute the strategy. In the case of the military, their lives depend on the quality of the dialogue between senior leadership and the team. Olympic teams face global public humiliation if they perform poorly — they may not win a medal, but sportscasters know their intended strategy and how well they execute against it. All these teams build on individual team member's strengths. There is no time to focus on weaknesses on the field of battle or on the ice. Weaknesses are built up into strengths in proactive development sessions utilizing simulations and follow-up coaching. Similarly, for business enterprises there is no time in today's crushing competitive environment to waste time not engaging in dialogue with each other and capitalizing on present strengths.

A culture of dialogue has, apparently, been evading some of the major players in the Pharma industry such as the Pfizer organization. Business Week reporter Arlene Weintraub (2006) states that Vice-Chairman Shedlarz, after being passed over for CEO, "got what might be an equally tough assignment". After the public humiliation of having to halt work on its most promising heart drug, Shedlarz "plans to shatter the barriers that have prevented several proud Pfizer units from functioning as a team". Pfizer is well known for its silo structure as well as military-like hierarchal structure. The article goes on to note that Wall Street greeted Pfizer's new plan to significantly reduce or eliminate their silo and hierarchical structure with a "yawn". APC would also yawn. It is not about structure, it is about culture. People must be willing to work with people who have very different world views, beliefs, and values. People must also be willing to set silo boundaries aside and set goals through dialogue as suggested by the Hay Group. Changes to structure without culture change is not likely to impact in any significant way Pfizer's ability to better execute its strategy. IBM and GE, discussed in Part I, had deep-seated hierarchal structures that permeated their identity. Both companies' senior leadership saw that this culture was not going to work for them. Yet as Miscovich (2003) notes "hierarchal corporate models, continue to dominate because, at their most basic level, they fulfill the human need for order, security, and identity" (p. 2). He goes on to state, as was also discussed in Part I, "GE, IBM, and Sony have succeeded by creating hybrid hierarchal systems with strong top–down values coupled with a more lateral structure for greater flexibility". Miscovich also makes a clear connection between performance improvement, SNA, and strategic learning. "Social Network mapping uncovers how people learn and who they learn from — important clues in understanding how the company actually functions" (p. 3).

APC and especially R&D intuitively formulated their strategy, operations, and culture in a way that would produce high levels of performance through strategic learning and leading change — culture change if needed. There was no doubt in the minds of senior leadership; culture change would be a top management priority. They would face the issues of time perception as our Derivative creators and BPR faced when they interacted with each other. They also would face cultural disconnects around strategy, operations, and structure. Cross-functional goal setting and collaboration would have to be actively managed by the senior team. They were committed to leading by example at the EC level. Before discussing APC's culture change strategy, we need to define what culture in today's business enterprise is.

What Is Culture

Deal and Kennedy (1982) popularized the concept of culture in business organizations. They defined culture as "the way we do things around here". Schein (1985) stated "culture is the way in which a group of people solve problems". Business executives were fascinated by this new lens or framework to understand why their strategy and operations were performing below expectations. Prior to both Deal and Kennedy and Schein, Hofstede (Hofstede, 1980, cited in Trompenaars, 1994) directly connected culture to organizational strategy, structure, priorities, and policies. Hofstede identified "mental programs" from which "people act out (behaviors) the meaning they get from their mental programs". This acting out results in organizational initiatives to be executed at high performance levels or not. Childress and Senn (1995) notes "The failure of many organizational improvement initiatives can generally be traced back to the corporate culture". These cultural failures are primarily responsible for individuals and teams to not learn from their experiences and, hence, not deliver on needed change. Culture enables strategic learning or not and strategic learning impacts culture.

Culture and Strategic Learning

Strategic learning has at its core the ability of individuals and teams to learn. Kasl et al. (1997) state "learning involves the interplay of individual and group values, beliefs, norms, knowledge, and behavior". Learning is culture in action. Teams through dialogue frame and reframe the problem to be solved or innovation needed. They experiment either through scenarios or take action to implement a solution or innovation. Through reflection and dialogue the team may create new knowledge that they use and also share with the larger organization. R&D often used the strategic learning process described in Chapter 5 to execute their strategy. Organizational strategy often anticipates changes in the way people work together to solve problems or to innovate (John, 1995). In Chapter 2, Strategic Outsourcing of Clinical Trials, a major change in strategic direction for APC produced both internal changes in the way people work together, as well as, working with external outsourcing partners.

A deeper impact on the organization's strategy is the effect culture has on shared values and beliefs that shape how individuals and teams think and act in their work processes. Kotter and Heskett (1992) emphasize that the founder or originating groups can often be long gone and people in the organization still operate within the strategic framework and structures set by them. Also, for global organizations, the originating group may be geographically distant and rarely, if ever, seen in person.

Culture change when discussed by Senior Leadership in very general terms often leads to more confusion in what to work on than clarity. Brion (2006) of Root Learning Systems notes "Business leaders often have trouble getting specific about the characteristics of the culture — values, beliefs, and behaviors they want to move to — and, of course, what they want to move away from". Culture change of any magnitude is a risky business and there are some cautions to be aware of.

Cautions on Culture Change

Leading successful execution efforts usually demands the effective management of change.

Hrebiniak (2005)

Hrebiniak cites the Gartner Group surveys and the Wharton Executive Education surveys both of which identity the inability to manage change as the single biggest obstacle to effective strategy execution. Culture change escalates the complexity of leading change many times over. Hrebiniak goes on to cite four major problem areas with organizations taking on complex change:

1. Coordination and managerial control are difficult to achieve when many tasks, activities have to be worked on in parallel.
2. Performance deviations are difficult to analyze in chaotic situations.
3. Lack of analysis in point 2 can lead to low levels of learning.
4. Performance standards may not be relaxed in times of complex change.

When you add the requirement that speed or urgency must be stepped up, performance levels of previously well-executed operations are likely to suffer. Everyone recognizes that culture impacts performance but Hrebiniak also cautions us to be aware of performance's impact on culture. He cites Motorola as a case in point. As Motorola lost market share in cell phones — a core competence — their CEO insisted on urgency as a priority and removed executives before they had a chance to respond to the requested cultural change — "we've got to get people who want to win and get a sense of urgency". The rest of the organization watched what was happening and spent precious time focusing on the wrong things. They took their eye off strategy execution at a time when it was critical to over deliver on the goals. Culture is a two way street — it is affected by performance and it affects performance.

APC navigated its way through the formulation of a new strategy, structure, and operating processes. They also believed their culture needed major change. Chapter 4 discussed the predecessor organizations — two medium-sized mediocre-performing companies who now aspired to dominate their industry — to accomplish this would require a very different kind of culture — a culture of high performance.

Leading the APC Culture Change

If we share a common understanding of our company's strategy and priorities, commit ourselves to exceeding our 2001 goals and continue to build a high performance culture, we will surely learn from our shortfalls and build significantly on our successes ... We will continue to build the culture of our company, especially in elevating the ability of the company to rapidly implement action plans.

CMO December (2001)

APC had more successes than failures as they were starting their third year of operations. Senior leadership realized that the culture, while still forming, needed to be addressed. The cultures had integrated remarkably well from 2000 to the end of 2001. An organic approach had been followed to date. Communications had planted the seeds of culture for employees at all levels, functions, and locations to know about and to become involved as they saw fit. The EC, at their November retreat, decided to take a proactive approach. Accelerating culture change (ACC) became an EC goal with a focus on two areas of the existing culture. By end of first quarter develop and propose an action plan to promote "sense of urgency" and "networking". Implement the plan as well as a measurement tool/survey (by second quarter) to track sense of urgency and networking. Each EC member, reporting actions taken and results achieved to the CMO was responsible for putting into operation the above goal. There were two parts to start the ACC initiative:

1. Drive the message into the organization that ACC, emphasizing sense of urgency and networking, is everyone's responsibility.
2. APC's priority for 2002 implies a special commitment from managers to coach all their employee's to live the sense of urgency and networking values.

The EC believed that a successful culture change initiative, across the organization, i.e. the global functions (R&D, Commercial, Manufacturing, and Support) and within the global high performing teams (GHPTs) so critical to APC's strategy, would show up as significantly improved strategy execution results. Success would be visible in individuals' and teams' behaviors. If strategic learning was a core capability of the organization it would be visible. A holistic and systemic approach would be needed to get everyone to understand what the culture change was about and why they should get on board.

Figure 7.1 captures the systemic approach from awareness to behavioral change. If successful, each function, country,

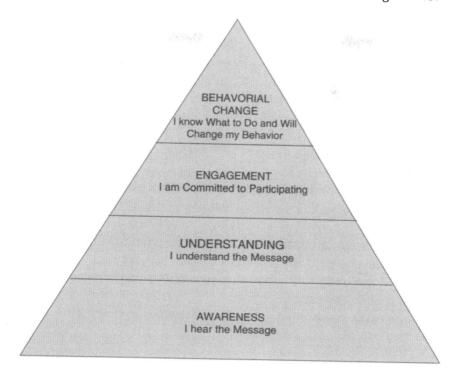

FIGURE 7.1 A Four Step Process for Living the Values.

(GHPT) could expect two outcomes:

1. Every employee would positively impact strategy execution efforts.
2. The APC strategy would be accepted by the financial community as being achievable.

APC was in the top 5 of Pharma companies in sales, yet their stock price was still below what it should have been given its placement in the industry. Stock analysts and investors were still not convinced that their global team-based strategy would work and deliver innovative new drugs faster than the traditional Pharma country strategy. APC after two years of operation still had a long way to go to prove itself and its new strategy for the industry.

R&D HR and GHR were asked by the EC to be point on the initiative in working with the global function heads. They went immediately to work with approximately three months to develop the plan and get EC agreement and then to implement by end of second quarter of 2002. The plan included the following elements:

1. Establish a clear definition of "networking" and "sense of urgency".
2. Articulate, refine, and agree upon the objectives of the initiative and the eventual measures of its success.
3. Develop a powerful, creative communications strategy to promote understanding and the importance of these two values.
4. Provide tools to enable employees to truly *live* networking and sense of urgency.
5. Measure the results of this initiative and determine the next steps.

Step 1 required clear and concise definitions of networking and sense of urgency:

1. Networking was defined as the ability to generate the most out of project-oriented, interdisciplinary teams that can work effectively together, eliminating barriers and exchanging knowledge seamlessly. External networking was encouraged with University Thought Leaders, professional associations as well as with strategic alliances with other Pharma organizations.
2. Sense of urgency was defined as developing and rewarding "smart speed" as an operational behavior. Smart speed is consistently keeping work as simple as possible without compromising product safety. Bureaucracy creep is eliminated whenever possible.

All employees would be responsible for living these two values of the ACC initiative. Managers would play a role institutionalizing these behaviors by first, modeling these behaviors themselves and second, holding their direct reports to this higher standard of behavior. The deployment team secured approval from the EC by the end of first quarter of 2002. They had less than 90 days to design, build, and deploy the initiative. Smart speed would be the order of the day.

The ACC team had a four-point approach:

1. Include ratings/measurements of urgency and networking as part of the Talent Management and Performance Management processes. HR professionals were trained to support and coach their functional managers in performing these roles as discussed in Chapter 4.
2. Develop and deploy a communication strategy that sustains interest.
3. Utilize Global Employee Opinion Survey and a web-based follow-up system to measure and track our progress.
4. Incorporate urgency and networking components into existing training programs as appropriate.

The Talent Management Review process was immediately modified to accommodate a discussion for all employees reviewed as below:

Rate each employee in the Talent Management database (Incumbents, Successors, and Future Leader candidates for key positions) using the four rating levels below for living urgency and networking.
a. Outstanding
b. Excellent
c. Meets Expectations
d. Partially Meets/Fails.

The message was clear. Employees who aspired to high potential (Future Leaders) designation needed to be visibly networking and utilizing "smart speed". Similarly, in the Performance Management process there was an assessment for urgency and networking included in the 2002 individual goal assessment area. This was part of the "Personal Leadership Dimension" (PLD) rating indicating how goals were met. The PLD was defined as living the values, especially sense of urgency and networking. Once again, a clear message from the EC. Performance Management directly impacted an employee's merit raise, bonus, and growth potential in the organization. Their overall evaluation now included a culture change element. The stakes were high and so every employee must be aware of the culture change initiative and its impact on them.

The global communications function was critical in preparing the organization for the change ahead. They would focus on:

1. Communication that enables employees to change their behavior, so they can live — not just understand — the message.
2. Establishing a communication system that is more than just a top–down cascade of information.
3. Explaining the external drivers for the internal change so that employees understand why the change is critical to business success.
4. Integrating communication into day-to-day work life, so it is not just a one-time event with short-term results.
5. Creative execution to heighten the interest and the engagement of employees.

The global communications function would execute their part of the deployment by:

1. Establishing communication linkages, e.g. to future Global Town Hall meetings, global employee survey reports, web and print updates, magazines, promotional pieces, etc.
2. Creating an Awards/Recognition program
   a. spot awards (at local/functional level) and
   b. Presidents Award Program (Global).

These awards would recognize individuals, but more importantly GHPTs that lived both networking and sense of urgency.

The deployment also incorporated networking and urgency into existing development programs. This would include all local, regional, and global (as discussed in Chapter 6) leadership development programs. The ALTs also had a just-in-time leadership development segment as discussed in Chapter 4. ALT facilitators would be trained to provide networking and urgency materials as well.

There were two components to follow-up and monitor progress in the culture change initiative. APC often utilized electronic pulsing technology to find out what employees were thinking/feeling about the organization — its strategy, operations, culture, and leadership/management teams. This pulse would be done globally with accommodation to the 20,000 manufacturing employees who did not have easy access to a computer. Kiosks were set up in break areas and they were given time from their work day to complete the pulse. The EC was committed to every employee participating in the accelerated culture change program.

The e-pulse consisted of the questions shown in Figure 7.2; four for networking and four for sense of urgency.

The results would be tabulated from the first e-pulse done at the end of second quarter of 2002 and the results reported out by the Chairman in one of his weekly columns to all employees. The second e-pulse would be done in first quarter of 2003 and the Presidents Award given at the Global Town Hall Meeting in April 2003. Employees had spoken through the pulse survey. APC was moving in the right direction but it was not doing so in all functions or countries. More effort would have to be made and urgently in these areas. Pulse feedback also indicated that some felt they were reinventing the wheel but they did not know enough about what other areas were doing until it was too late.

To provide continuous support and minimize duplicative efforts, the ACC designed a virtual Community of Values

	To a Very Great Extent	Quite A Bit	Some-what	A Little	Not At All	Don't Know/Not Applicable
SENSE OF URGENCY						
-Takes action in a timely manner	1	2	3	4	5	6
-Keeps work as simple as possible	1	2	3	4	5	6
-Strives to eliminate unnecessary bureaucracy	1	2	3	4	5	6
-Consistently delivers results	1	2	3	4	5	6
NETWORKING						
-Freely shares information and ideas beyond department/functional boundaries	1	2	3	4	5	6
-Treats co-workers as partners, not competitors	1	2	3	4	5	6
-Effectively builds collaboration and teamwork; breaks down silos	1	2	3	4	5	6
-Strives to do what is best for the company (not just one's unit)	1	2	3	4	5	6

FIGURE 7.2 Being Carried Out in Practice.

website that would provide information, tools, and other support:

- Definitions of each of the values and the associated behaviors. See Table 7.1 for details on all seven APC values.
- An on-line meeting template or other communal activities to set goals for individual departments on how to translate these values into real actions for specific departments and specific jobs.
- Electronic bulletin boards to share thoughts about how different departments are implementing these values.
- A "test" to self-assess how effective an individual is at living these values.

The Community of Values website would become part of the High Performance Organization (HPO) intranet website that would be deployed in 2002. The HPO website provided a

TABLE 7.1 APC Values

Respect for People — demonstrated by developing people; creating a meritocracy in which performance is rewarded; respect for people of different national, cultural, racial, and corporate backgrounds.

Integrity — reaching the right decisions; transparency in our actions, motives, and intentions.

Sense of Urgency — speed and simplicity in everything we do; goal oriented and delivering results; fighting bureaucracy; think about our processes and change the barriers and structures to reduce friction.

Networking — reaching out beyond internal boundaries not just to get information and ideas but to share our ideas and information with colleagues. Breaking down silos. Going outside our organization to expand our network base.

Creativity — looking for innovation in all processes and everything we do. It means embracing the discomfort we feel moving into unknown territory.

Empowerment — creating an environment in which people know we expect them to have the self-confidence to show initiative and be accountable for the results.

Courage — openly challenging and discussing processes, decisions, and strategy goals. Setting demanding targets for ourselves and others to achieve.

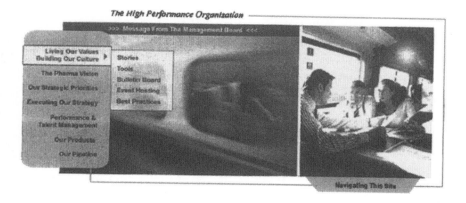

FIGURE 7.3 The HPO Website.

common virtual space for all employees. Figure 7.3 highlights the sections on the site that provided key EC messages, financial results, guidelines, tools, etc. around APC values, vision, strategy, performance/rewards, talent management, and products/pipeline. The work of GHPTs in specific product areas would be accessible to all. Most importantly, all employees could track the progress the organization was making on the accelerated culture change initiative.

As 2003 came to a close, the Head of GHR stated:

Our role is to align our people with the strategic goals and objectives of the company in order to develop an organizational culture that embraces performance, innovation, and flexibility ... Our business leaders have accepted us as strategic business partners ... We are fully committed to meeting the challenges that lie ahead.

APC would be acquired in 2004 by a Pharma that, while very successful, believed the Country Managed organization strategy to be the strategy of choice. Almost all of what APC created is gone, such as the Global Team-Based Organization strategy, the GHPTs (cross-functional), and the global leadership development curriculum. In the new organization, country efforts are coordinated by a small but capable global staff. In R&D, their global and cross-functional approach to strategy communication and some of the knowledge sharing platforms are gone. The new leadership looked at each of the R&D platforms and determined if it fit into their country-based strategy. The HPO website no longer exists. Fortunately, Strategic Learning and Leading Change are alive and well in the new organization. Strategic learnings are collected at the product level within a country and shared with other countries on a more informal basis than APC's global structure. Informal Networking across country lines has become very important to the new organization. Countries report learnings and requests for needed change to a global coordinator for their functional area who in turn shares this with other functional coordinators and the Management Committee for action. In some respects this restores the traditional Pharma strategy of silos and hierarchy that we saw Pfizer is committed to changing. It remains to be seen if senior leadership can successfully sustain a global business using this approach. Tom, our diabetic patient, is in very good hands. The new company's diabetes drug portfolio is the envy of the industry. Many of the APC people stayed with the new company. The company's purpose remains the same — to discover innovative drugs that improve peoples' health and bring them to the patient in a shorter lifecycle than the traditional industry standard.

HR at the global functional level and at the global corporate level played a strategic role in creating APC from two medium-sized, mediocre-performing Pharma companies in 1999. HR had to reinvent itself to earn and keep its seat at the EC table. Other organizations in other industries have also reinvented themselves. Part III discusses several such companies and their experience in earning their seat at the CEO's table.

References

Brion, A. Conversation About Root Learning Systems, Experience Working with Global Organizations and Culture Change, 2006.

Childress, J. R., and Senn, L. E. *In the Eye of the Storm: Reengineering Corporate Culture.* LA/NY: The Leadership Press, 1995.

Deal, T. E., and Kennedy, A. A. *Corporate Cultures.* Reading, MA: Addison Wesley, 1982.

Hay Group. "Managing Performance: Achieving Outstanding Performance through a 'Culture of Dialogue.'" Working Papers, Hay Group Research conducted by K. Lemaire and L. Reissman, 2002.

Hofstede, G. *Cultures, Consequences.* London: Sage, 1980, cited in Trompenaars, F. *Riding the Waves of Culture: Understanding Diversity in Global Business.* London: Irwin, 1994.

Hrebiniak, L. G. *Making Strategy Work: Leading Effective Execution and Change.* Philadelphia, PA: Wharton School Publishing, 2005.

John, S. "A Study of Team Learning in a Professional Services Company." Doctoral Dissertation, Columbia University, 1995.

Kasl, E., Marsick, V. J., and Dechant, K. "Teams as Learners: A Research Based Model of Team Learning." *Journal of Applied Behavioral Science* 33 (1997): 227–246.

Kotter, J. P., and Heskett, J. L. *Corporate Culture and Performance.* New York: The Free Press, 1992.

Miscovich, P. J. *The New Knowledge Workplace.* White Paper, PWC, NY.

Schein, E. *Organizational Culture and Leadership.* San Francisco, CA: Jossey-Bass, 1985.

Weintraub, A. "The Big Rethink at Pfizer: After a Heart Drug Debacle, It's Reassessing the Way it Bets on Unproven Technology." *Business Week, News & Insights,* December 18, 2006.

III

HOW GLOBAL COMPANIES ARE REINVENTING HUMAN RESOURCES

This part examines the role of the Human Resources function in today's global organizations. Some business commentators and business leaders have expressed little confidence in HR living up to everyone's expectations. Chapter 8 presents several examples of companies that are earning the respect of the CEO's team and earning their seat as business partners at the strategy table. Also discussed are the critical business strategy capabilities needed by today's HR function. The chapter provides a sure fire method of earning your seat — the 100 Day Commitment. An Epilogue closes the book. My personal reflections and learning on a career that spans over 25 years in Organizational Effectiveness and Executive Development are explored.

8

Reinventing Human Resources

I want you to know that the seat is there. Let there be no doubt in anybody's mind. If you are not getting the seat, don't say the seat is not there. Instead, question why you are not getting the seat.

Charan (2006)

The "seat" Charan is referring to is, of course, the one at the CEO's table. A seat at the table means being a strategic partner adding visible and measurable value to the organization. At a time when there is unprecedented change impacting organizations, especially those that are global or are in the process of globalizing — voluntarily or otherwise. There is chaos and complexity in every facet of business and society. Fickle consumers who change brands at will, regulatory agencies that often stop product launches without detailed explanations, employees from different countries, as well as generations, having very different ideas of what constitutes an ideal employment situation are among the most visible challenges facing an organization's leadership team. Less visible, but nevertheless dangerous to the long-term health of an organization are competitors. Competitors utilize business intelligence techniques (legal) to gather data, analyze it, and make needed changes to their strategy, operations, and/or culture. Many companies today fear unknown competitors. Financial Service firms call this phenomena disintermediation.

Who is out there to steal your customers that you are totally unaware of? An example in the Financial Services industry occurred in the 1990s when the Dutch government held an auction for the sale of financial instruments. This innovative way to sell these instruments to wholesale purchasers versus individuals took the Financial Services industry by complete surprise. The fact that this was done through a government supported organization was even more startling, particularly to U.S. centric organizations.

Many organizations, over the past 10–15 years, have adapted to the speed and complexity of change. This resilience has often led to large-scale organizational changes that have made some organizations less than desirable places to work and to build a career. Those organizations that have managed to change their strategy and operations into high-performance cultures and, also cultures that people want to work in have gone to the number one or two place in their industry. These organizations consistently won the war for customers and talent. Unfortunately, the HR function has not adapted so well. HR "seems stuck" in its past as described by Hammonds (2005) and Stern (2006) below. In its Personnel days the function acted as the enforcer of policies and got in the way of business leaders executing the strategy.

HR to the Rescue or Not

The meeting was not starting off so well. APC's Global Head of HR had been asked to come to discuss "some HR issues" with the Global Head of Strategic Alliances. The Strategic Alliance function is a very powerful and important function to the long-term success of the company. The Global Head of Strategic Alliances exerted significant influence with his peers on the Management Committee.

Before he was seated he said "You know what's wrong with you HR guys?" And without stopping said, "Let me tell you. You don't add upfront value. We ask you to identify the people issues with a proposed strategy change and we get back policy mumbo jumbo. We ask for a list of high potentials and the possible positions they can fill this year and next and we get back — 'the system isn't easy to work with to get that info quickly'. We get nothing strategic that helps us evaluate the next big deal we are thinking about, the people stuff. After the deal is done, you come around with the you coulda, shoulda, woulda done stuff. Sorry to be so blunt but it's been eating away at me for quite a while".

Another unsatisfied customer of HR. It is been almost two decades since HR started transforming itself. Competency models for generalists and specialists. Lots of different HR structures have been tried over those two decades. Yet many business leaders feel HR will never earn the "seat" that Charan refers to.

Hammonds (2005), in his cover story, Why We Hate HR, states "HR is the corporate function with the greatest potential — the key driver, in theory, of business performance — and also the one that most consistently under-delivers". He goes on to say "most HR organizations have ghettoized themselves literally to the brink of obsolescence. They are competent at the administrivia of pay, benefits, and retirement, but companies increasingly are farming out those functions ... What's left is the more important strategic role of raising the reputation and intellectual capital of the company — but HR is, it turns out, uniquely unsuited for that".

On the other side of "the pond", a similar article appeared. Stern (2006) states "without finance there are not accounts to file and no commercial record of performance ... But take away the human resources department and what? ... how much would your company actually suffer?" He goes on to note "less than 10 per cent of FTSE100 companies have an HR director on the board. The truth is the profession is at a crisis point, with its credibility — and future — at stake". Stern refers to Ulrich's 1997 book — Human Resources Champions — as a "pathway to salvation". Ulrich's four-pillar approach has been lauded by many HR professional and some business leaders as the way to that "seat" at the table. Stern notes the wide difference of opinion between HR executives and business leaders. A Price Waterhouse Coopers (PWC) (UK) survey cites 73 percent of HR Directors see their role as strategic. PWC also found that 51 percent of CEOs look at the HR function primarily as "an administrative centre". Ulrich, in his four-pillar approach to HR, says HR professionals need to be: administrative experts, strategic partners, change agents, and employee champions. The UK executives cited by PWC and, certainly, APC's Global Head of Strategic Alliances would agree that there is a disconnection between Ulrich's four pillars and the HR professionals they interact with on a daily basis. No doubt the business and social challenges that are part of today's competitive environment has made it difficult for many HR functions and professionals to be strategic and add measurable value to their organization. There are some examples — more and more each year of strategic HR functions as we see below.

HR to the Rescue: For Real

The "seat" at the table for HR, as a strategic business partner is needed in global organizations. These organizations cannot wait 10–15 years for HR to become unstuck and assume a leadership role. Only a handful of companies are cited as having their Senior HR Officer at the business strategy table. GE, Pitney Bowes, Goldman Sachs, Proctor and Gamble, and Cardinal Health are among those most often mentioned. Recent newcomers to the club:

1. Yahoo — Libby Sartain, Chief People Officer, has Talent Development at the top of the COO's weekly meeting. The message is clear to the organization — employees understand that development is a core value and HR professionals understand that their roles are not paper pushing administrivia. Sartain says (quoted in Hammonds, 2005) "We view human resources as the caretaker of the largest

investment in the company". Yahoo has enormous business challenges ahead of it. Google has leapfrogged everyone in the industry sector and is committed to keeping their competitive advantage. Google started searching for a Global Head of Organization Development (OD) and Leadership Development. A major concern of theirs and all global companies is that without a shared core leadership capability, the company culture is in danger of fragmenting and wasting precious time to market with new/innovative products. Also as acquisitions are made, renegade cultures can dominate the environment and the small company soul they want to preserve will be lost. To this end, they have brought on a Head of HR from a best practice company who in turn is building a strategic GHR function.

2. Best Buy (BB) — Two courageous women in HR decided to do something positive about BB's face time culture. They wanted to change the culture to a "Results-Only Work Environment". Conlin notes "Cynics thought it was a PR stunt dreamed up by Machiavellian operatives in human resources" (p. 63). This was not a top–down CEO mandated initiative. As Conlin (2006) states, "It was a covert guerilla action that spread virtually and eventually became a revolution. So secret was the operation that the CEO only learned the details two years after it began transforming his company. The essence of the program is that employees make their own work-life decisions. The HR duo shielded the initiative from enemies until the results started showing up in the numbers. Average rise in worker productivity — those in the program — 35 percent. Voluntary turnover is down substantially as well — (−52 percent) for logistics as an example. They utilized the BB social network to spread the word. The ultimate business accolade was awarded to these Strategic Learning/culture change agents — the CEO formed a for-profit business subsidiary called Culture Rx to assist other companies in going "clock less", i.e. no fixed work hours or schedules, only results.

3. International Harvester (Navistar) — an old line (1902) industrial company specializing in engines. The transformation led by a visionary HR Executive, started in 1999 has survived/now flourishing even with a new CEO taking over in 2004. Navistar faced a number of serious marketplace challenges. They were considered a solid reliable engine producer, but not an innovative one. The marketplace is seeking solutions that are environmentally friendly and socially responsible. They faced a number of people strategy-related challenges as well. Sixty percent of their leadership/management would be retiring in less than 3 years. They wanted to be considered a preferred employer, but employee and recruiting feedback told them they were not even close. Diversity candidates saw that they were not a diversity friendly company. Employees told them (through surveys) that the old guard was not open to new ideas, new ways of doing things, and there was no high-quality Learning and Development program for career building. Navistar HR approached their transformation in three areas:

a. Performance and Promotability Assessment — They created a common leadership profile across the organization through which Performance Evaluations were driven and 360 assessments utilized. Overall performance evaluation was based on innovation delivered, diversity goals, and current work goals.

b. Talent Pipeline — focused effort on high-potential identification and accelerated development, quarterly talent reviews, rotational assignments, 100 day transition strategy, and support moving to new positions or rotations.

c. Monitoring the culture change — regular electronic pulsing was conducted on how well leadership was doing in building a company that was considered innovative and that diverse candidates would be attracted to and stay.

These pulses showed substantial progress in moving from a negatively perceived place to work and grow to an organization that recognized capabilities in a fair, consistent, and credible way.

4. Arthur Andersen

As the 1990s started, Arthur Andersen (AA) formed a task force, which they named AA21, to identify the challenges and suggest solutions for AA to prosper into the 21st century.

AA would need to define and implement a People Strategy that was comparable to their business strategy — i.e., create both a high-performing organization (HPO) and employer of choice (EOC) firm. By excelling at both elements (HPO and EOC), the firm would significantly improve its overall strategy execution capability and reap tremendous economic rewards. An EOC culture would enable the firm to build the talent pipeline needed to promote partners sufficiently experienced to interact with senior executives at large client organizations. This EOC culture would have to be strong enough to reverse the trend of new recruits leaving the firm in droves within 3 years of their joining the firm. New recruits out of the universities were looking for exciting work, which AA provided. However, they were also looking for a firm that would enable them to balance their work and personal life. They were not willing to completely sacrifice their personal life for a partnership opportunity approximately 14 years away.

One key element of having an EOC culture was to create a membership feeling for employees. Practice Communities (PC) were formed as the core component of building a membership culture. Support and active participation by senior partners would ensure successful deployment of the PCs. A media-based communications campaign also gave tangible support to these PCs. Finally,

HR directors and managers were trained to coach and counsel the PC leaders as well as community members. HR also shared lessons learned within their community with other communities. Success was tracked using email "pulses", i.e., short, focused questions on employee satisfaction with the firm as a result of the PC initiative. As a result of the PC initiative, employees stayed on the job longer because they felt connected to their community. They could surface professional and work/life issues as well as interact with regional leadership and see change occur as a direct result of their community. AA dissolved as a result of the Enron scandal, however, rumor has it that at least one audit community continues to connect people to each other and support each other in times of adversity as well as happiness. It is also rumored that some communities have split into smaller communities and continue their community building even though the firm is gone. It seems members of these communities have learned both the power of community and the skills and tenacity to have their community endure in face of incredible negative forces, which by all accounts, should have killed the community when AA collapsed as a result of the Enron scandal.

In addition to the PC, the task force sought input from AA partners and employees as well as external thought leaders who were experts in organizational strategy and tactics. The task force posed a straightforward question: The approach of the 21st century will require that organizations significantly improve their strategy formulation and execution capability — What must AA do to meet the strategy execution challenges of the 21st century? To minimize internal conflict and politics, the task force contracted qwith a world-recognized consulting firm in working with organizations to improve strategy execution capability. The study designed and conducted by the external consulting organization had two primary objectives: (1) identify and define the current and projected issues facing AA in executing its strategic vision, and (2) define the role of the global, country, and regional HR functions in supporting the AA strategic vision. The task force reported:

"We have completed our task force study and are now ready to pilot a strategy that we believe will help us strengthen HR throughout AA ... What follows provides you with a substantive overview of what we have learned and where we are headed ... World-class HR holds an important key to issues of employee satisfaction, which is directly linked to client satisfaction and to our ability to meet and exceed our growth and profit goals. In short world-class HR links the four cornerstones" which were Exceeding Client Expectations, Best People and Fulfilling Work Environment, Growth and Market Share, and Quality Risk Management (Extract from memo from *Global HR Managing Partner*, November 1995).

AA found itself at a crossroads. Revenues and profits were soaring. To compete for the best people required to fuel growth, AA must demonstrate its ability to:
- Offer outstanding professional opportunities for people with a wide variety of skills,
- Be the *employer* of choice for all demographic groups, and
- Operate globally in meeting the needs of its people.

AA must achieve the above within a context of government regulation and competition for people with firms who are bringing their own HR management into line with business realities.

The task force also noted the gap between the current HR management model and the current operating context as significant. The Business Unit suffers as a result.
- There is no formal HR strategy, developed with and designed to support business strategy. Relevant HR considerations are not deliberated in tandem with strategic business issues.

- HR issues are not identified and resolved in a systematic fashion.
- AA is not doing an adequate job of retaining the best people.
- Most locations view HR people as administrators only.
- HR people must usually depend on line partners to champion their initiatives and effect their implementation.
- Partners are overburdened with tasks that could be handled by people with specific HR expertise.
- Line personnel, especially partners, do not get the assistance they need to address the HR issues effectively.
- HR capabilities are not adequate for providing the level of service and support suitable to a worldwide, world-class organization, and they are inconsistent from location to location.
- Most HR people do not have the skills or tools they need to provide a high level of professional, value-added service to their "clients" within AA.

None of the requirements for effective competition for the best people can be met with the current structure and mode of managing human resources.

Requirements for acquiring and retaining the best people are:

- A strong, credible HR function, serving in a consultative/ strategic rather than merely administrative capacity will remedy these problems. The new role for the HR function is to position HR professionals as "trusted business advisors" to line management.
- People management remains a line management responsibility.

The firm's Board of Partners agreed that a key step to implementing the Task Forces findings was to fix the HR structure as a first step. Each region was authorized to formally set up a partner-level HR position for their region and a partner or director of HR position for larger local offices as well. The Board of Partners, however, did not mandate this change, but rather, recommended it. Each Regional Managing Partner was free to accept the change or reject it.

AA had come close to implementing a GHR strategy and structure by 1995. A partnership governance structure is set up so that each partner has an equal vote and global changes needed to receive a majority vote. The effectiveness of the HR function was not an issue for many countries in the firm and as a result the vote did not receive a majority and implementation became a regional decision. The US decided to proceed with implementing the strategic HR design starting in the US firm's largest region — Metro NY. AA was ahead of its time but even the visionary leadership that created the AA21 Task Force could not foresee the troubles that would lie ahead for the firm-Enron.

Arthur Andersen material is based on previously published work — John (2004).

APC discussed in Part I and II was also building a new kind of GHR function. Their primary focus for the first 2 years of the integration was consulting to the line on strategy execution and culture building. In years 3 and 4, the focus shifted to building a GHR structure and deepening their HR professionals' capabilities to deliver business function requests. The EC gave them a seat at the table from day one but they had to earn their seat over and over again. HR got their seat because the EC believed that you have to trust first and then you can ask to be trusted. After 4 years, even the most jaded business leader admitted HR had earned their seat at the strategy table. For many firms it is still a struggle or a distant possibility. Earning your seat at the table under circumstances where trust levels are low is discussed next.

Earning Your Seat at the Table

Globalization, as we saw in Parts I and II, has created an interesting dilemma for business and HR leaders. It has produced an environment where revolutionary speed is needed along with flexibility to effectively execute strategy. Yet few of us are capable of performing at these speeds for sustained periods of time without support from our organizations. This support, in the knowledge economy, often takes the form of coaching and facilitating teams as they align their goals to strategy and prepare to execute. The HR function, when effective, is well positioned to enable individuals and teams to reach/attain peak performance and development. Ulrich (1997), Fitz Enz (1997), and Walker (1992) have studied and consulted to organizations extensively about the characteristics of an effective HR function. These characteristics/capabilities are:

1. Administrative effectiveness across all HR Processes and systems for recruitment, On-Boarding, compensation and benefits, performance management/rewards, talent management, and employee's development/career building.
2. Employee Champions, i.e. as voice to senior leadership and management across a wide range of employees areas such as identifying employee expectations regarding their current and future roles within the organization and representing employees when needed on administrative matters such as work permits and short-term job relocation assignments.
3. Agents of Change, i.e. acting as role models for both senior leadership, management, and employees when the strategic direction, structure, operating processes, or culture changes and all are expected to get on board quickly with the new way of doing things.

Huselid et al. (2005) have found that highly effective HR functions are key members of the CEO's strategy team. Their role is identifying the implications to the workforce capabilities and behaviors needed for the strategy to be executed or the revised strategy based on past strategy execution efforts. In addition, experience tells us that HR must also be capable of assessing the changes to organizational structure, operating processes and culture, and recommending/leading specific changes in these areas. This is the "seat at the table discussed above and must be earned given HRs historical level of performance in all the above areas.

Earning a "seat" at the table is not easy by any means. Years, and in some cases decades of negative perceptions about HR are not going to vanish overnight. Especially in an environment where only a handful of companies are ever mentioned as having their HR Head at the business strategy table. HR needs a strategy and then the courage to execute it at the speed of light. The alternative is/if not HR will be outsourced in its entirety. Business units will only buy services that add value and pay accordingly. Commodity outsourcing, discussed in Part I, hit HR a long time ago. Payroll and parts of Compensation and Benefits were the first to be outsourced. Some outsourcing firms developed a model to manage Training and Development with mixed results. It would not be long before other specialty areas like Organizational Development will be outsourced. The outsourcing of most or all of HR is not a given. HR can rescue itself. There is no one else who can or will.

If you ask anyone of the major consulting firms for a proposal on transforming HR, you will receive a minimum of 50 slides and, most likely, 75 or more. The focus will be on developing a very tightly constructed project management approach to the transformation. The scope of the transformation as well as approach and deliverables will be displayed in beautifully colored power point slides. Roles and responsibilities with next steps will be clearly documented. Some may throw in a generic HR competency model for discussion about HR building long-term relationships with their client bases — "the business leaders and their teams". What is most likely missing is a clear picture of how HR professionals will apply their know how in specific areas as Charan (2006) suggests is necessary to earn the "seat" at the table. Instead there will be a heavy focus on the structure, including org charts of the new

HR. Most likely business leaders will yawn and go back to executing their strategy as best as possible. The HR transformation plan will have little or no focus on the changes that are surfacing for the business and specifically how HR will work with the strategy execution teams. No real discussions about how those changes impact their talent and how leadership development could prepare them for the future. Nor will there be any substantive discussions about the culture and its impact on their efforts. Many HR transformation efforts focus entirely on a new structure and capability profiles for HR professionals and not with meeting the expectations of the business leaders and the strategy execution teams.

Frank Capra's classic movie (1947) — It's a Wonderful Life — shows us the world with George Bailey and, then, without him. With HR at the table it can be a very different world for the global organization. HR professionals, whether Generalist or Specialist, must be capable of delivering three services:

1. Working with business and support teams to effectively set goals that, if delivered, will execute their part of the strategy above expectations. HR professionals must be embedded in these teams before, during, and after execution efforts. APC accomplished this with HR/KM (Knowledge Management) Consultants and the R&D One Page Strategy sessions discussed in Chapter 5.

2. Understanding industry conditions that may, in the short term, trigger changes in an organization's strategic direction. HR professionals must be able to translate these anticipated changes into assisting teams with goals/ deliverables changes and identifying capabilities that may be scarce or missing in the organization today and how these might be developed in time to enable the revised strategy to be executed at a high-performance level. We saw in Chapter 2, how APC changed its strategy quickly to respond to industry conditions by outsourcing its clinical trials. The senior HR professional was taken by surprise. As a result, he thought he was delivering quick,

high-quality service to the unit head when he immediately posted the Manager of Strategic Outsourcing job in the external search website. HR report card — speed of service warrants an A; impact on current employee's career building/representing best interests of employees warrants an F. Ulrich (1997) reminds us clearly of HRs role in being an employee advocate. The HR professional would have served the organization leadership and its employees more effectively if he had asked questions and gotten answers. Questions such as – how will this change in strategic direction impact our high-potential talent, who may be displaced or have their career paths modified? What will we, as an organization, do for these people? Answers to these fundamental questions in advance of the change in organizational strategy and structure would create a very different culture.

3. Leading Culture Change

Standard social and business practices are built on certain assumptions — shared understanding that have evolved from older beliefs and conditions. And while circumstances may have changed since the start of these practices, their continued use tends to reconfirm the old beliefs. For this reason our daily practices feel right and true to us, regardless of whether they have evolved to keep up with the pace of change. In just such a way a business culture arises and perpetuates itself, perhaps long after its usefulness has passed.

Zander (2000)

Louis V. Gerstner, Jr. former Head of IBM and no stranger to change has said publicly a number of times — "Culture isn't just one aspect of the game — it is the game". As we saw in Parts I and II, there is no "cookie-cutter" approach to being an effective change agent. For instance, BB, described above, utilized guerilla warfare-like approach similar to what we might see in action movies. In real life we see Military Special

Operations teams maneuvering their way through hostile terrain, shielding themselves from their enemies. The HR culture change team waited until they had visible successes and business leader/employee support in an area before moving to another area. Navistar chose a more conservative approach and one that shared the prospective culture change with the organization as a whole. They started with top–down support. Very different approaches based on understanding the context of culture and the depth of change being asked of the culture. BB was shattering the "way we do things around here" at the core of the organization's belief system. Less dramatic, but nonetheless difficult was Navistar's depth of change being asked for. Diversity of recruitment and promotion in an industry setting dominated by men for almost 100 years was not an easy change to bring into reality. Strong, successful cultures sometimes recognize the need to change their culture. They may call in their HR Head to discuss and perhaps support an external consulting firm or assist in the hiring of an executive who "can shake things up around here". Berner (2007) covers the public firing of Roehm at Wal-Mart after 10 months as a culture change agent. Roehm, a marketing whiz at Daimler-Chrysler states "[Wal-Mart] would rather have a painkiller [than] taken the vitamin of change". Culture change for anyone is never easy. There are promising change tools like SNA discussed in Chapter 3. Communities of Practice can be invaluable in supporting culture change in its early days and providing a forum for sustaining the change. APC utilized both tools to their advantage. SNA is useful in surfacing internal thought leaders and other "influential's" who may not show up prominently on the organization chart. When HR professionals utilize strategic learning tools, they can identify these influentials and, later, enlist their support for the change. Also in facilitating performance management goal setting and results feedback/coaching for execution teams, the HR professional is in a position to recommend specific changes that will impact the team's performance. When a team can connect change, even culture change, to performance impact, the change may be more easily embraced especially if rewards in addition to bonuses include high-potential recognition with accelerated development as well. Changes needed in an organization that are more long term in nature present challenges to a culture change agent, i.e. there is little appetite for people to change when a short term crisis is absent. The Strategic Alliance concept, that many organizations embrace today, to increase execution efforts, provides techniques and tools for the culture change agent's use. Many Alliances, like mergers/acquisitions, fail to deliver full value to the parties. Often there are culture clashes between the companies as discussed in Chapter 2 — Strategic Outsourcing. As a result of lessons learned in building alliances, many global organizations develop relationship building, negotiation, and conflict resolution skills for employees working in alliances. APC built in just-in-time development into alliance teams from early formation to disbanding. The debriefing for strategic learning's from such APC alliances yielded the following — both company's alliance members felt deeply connected to the alliance but for different cultural reasons. One company's team representatives felt deeply connected because of the defined team structure and roles while the other company's team representatives felt deeply connected because of the quality of the dialogues around problems and innovations. Culture is truly in the eye of the beholder.

Fitz Enz (1990) notes "Never in its history has the human resources department had such opportunity to affect organizational change". He also cites Robert Townsend, a business author, "In my first book, I said get rid of the personnel department. Then you changed the name to Human Resources. In my next book, I am going to say, get rid of HR". Fast forward to the 21st century and Hammonds (2005) takes on both Fitz Enz and Townsend's persona and beliefs about HR and what its fate will be. HR must take charge of its destiny or someone else will. Whatever HR commits to as reinventing itself it must be done at warp speed. There is a large amount of cynicism in the business community at large about HR and any delays would only increase the negative feelings.

The 100 Day Commitment

Never was there a time when the Kiss model (Keep It Simple Stupid) is more needed. Senior leadership and management levels have not shown a lot of interest in organizational research and theory. London (2006) states "many working managers view consumption of management theory — even in digested form — as largely a waste of time". For example, when a business team asks HR for a team-building intervention, it often leads to frustration for the team. HR has adopted a beautifully elegant conceptual model of how effective teams should work. They then doggedly apply the model to the team intervention. Every area of the model has to be covered in sequence without deviation. Often the team is looking for a fresh set of eyes to help them debrief lessons learned and going forward suggestions to improve their performance. They are not looking at the workplace equivalent of the movie Groundhog Day. The strategic learning approach covered in Chapter 3 served APC well in a variety of settings. When there were deep-seated team formation/performance problems, they were worked utilizing standard OD techniques such as interviews and assessment instruments. In recent years, organizations have been providing leaders in transition support. This support consists of a 100 day plan (90 if you follow Watkins, 2003) to be developed by the new leader and supported by the organization. The purpose of the plan is to ensure an effective transition from one role to another, one level to a higher level or for leaders joining the organization from another external organization. The premise is that, if you follow the plan, you achieve high performance and acceptance by the new culture you are about to enter. The HR function, in a number of global organizations, has supported this approach to fast tracking individual leaders.

Bradt et al. (2006) identifies three conceptual frameworks underpinning their approach:

1. High-performing teams and organizations are built of people, plans, and practices aligned around a shared purpose.

2. Tactical capacity bridges the gap between strategy and execution, ensuring that a good strategy does not fail because of bad execution.
3. Five building blocks underpin a team's tactical capacity: a *burning imperative*, key *milestones*, *early wins*, getting the right people in the right *roles*, and shaping the *culture* with an ongoing communication plan.

HR could easily adapt this approach to earning their seat at the table. There is no more burning imperative than working with a business team to significantly improve its strategy execution. Secondly, commit to identifying a near term trend that will have Talent Management (Career Growth and/or Leadership Development) implications and have the curriculum changed to meet the identified trend. Finally, before a second 100 days occur identify one area of the culture and have an early win/success by changing the culture in the area. It can be a small item that irritates many people, e.g. a policy that requires four original signatures moves to electronic signatures or reduce the number to three signatures. It does not have to be a sacred cow in the culture to be changed to affect employees positively. Seeing the leadership move a change, however small, through the organization to completion is energizing at a time when most employees believe nothing changes — at least for the better.

By committing to the 100 day plan outlined above, HR can quickly establish or reestablish itself as a value adding function. The plan would be very straightforward and when accomplished give everyone in the organization hope that more and more good things would be coming out of HR in the near future. HR in today's environment would be committing suicide to try to design and implement a complicated reinvention. An example of such a plan is provided in Figure 8.1. This 100 day plan has HR leading the change effort for deploying an already designed LSP that by the end of 100 days becomes embedded into recruiting, performance

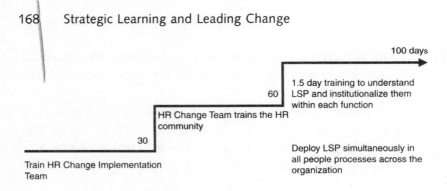

FIGURE 8.1 Change Management: 100 Day Plan.

management/rewards, talent management, and leadership development. More senior HR professionals are trained first by the Org Effectiveness department and/or consulting firm that partnered with the organization to build the LSP. These HR professionals then train the remaining HR community so that the inevitable questions from managers and employees can be handled by anyone in HR. The HR professional, i.e. the contact person with line managers, then leads the change into each function. No doubt the timeline is very tight but can be accomplished if HR works as a team as well as a community. Successfully deploying the LSP in this way can reestablish the trust in HR to deliver not only what it has promised but also what is so disparately needed by line managers and employees.

None of this will matter, if you do not have passion for your company's mission and vision. When APC's team shaved 18 months off manufacturing, it energized the entire company. It was not because the supply chain was going to be positively impacted. All employees could relate to Tom, our diabetic patient, who would have a higher quality of life earlier than if APC had not succeeded in their goal. APC did not live to see all its possibilities become reality. APC business leaders did experience the impact of an HR function that had a seat at the table. Those that did will never forget their experience.

The Chairman at an internal global business leader's conference at the end of 2003 stated:

> *Our competition envies our global team strategy and more importantly our results. Our execution capability is destined to become the standard of the industry ... we couldn't have gotten there so quickly without our HR colleagues support and dedication ...*

APC HR had a straightforward recipe for being seen as an effective department. First, they worked tirelessly with the top 200 to ensure that the basic HR processes worked at acceptable levels very early in the integration of the two companies. They took this effort beyond "administrivia" to include recruiting, performance management/rewards, talent management, and leadership development processes as well. Second, they did not rest on their laurels but sought continuous feedback from managers and employees utilizing surveys/pulses and reported out results to the entire organization in usable formats for immediate action. The EC made it clear that immediate action was required of all people and not just select functions or managers. Finally, HR championed the strategic learning processes and coached managers and teams to lead the changes that the learnings called for. It was not uncommon for senior business leaders to note that HR modeled the way within their own business unit. It was not to do as I say but do as I do.

Every industry and every company has the potential to provide valuable products/services to society. For example, the cigarette company that educates young people not to smoke. There is the candy company that publicly promises to not target children below 12 years of age in its advertising campaign. Corporate Social Responsibility, a relatively new role for corporations, is steadily gaining in importance. Many employees are looking for responsible Corporations that engage their passions. These corporations give back to their communities. Only high-performing companies can sustain their operations and be socially responsible. It is clear that HR has a major role to play, a leadership role to play in every organization and particularly those that are global. HR must take ownership for strategic learning and leading change initiatives in strategy, operations, and culture. This is "what really works" as we found out in Chapter 2. If HR also impacts Talent Management and Leadership Development, organizations will grow more and more powerful each day. We will create the organization that engages people's minds and hearts. It is our responsibility to do so.

An effective HR function is up to HR to create and sustain. We are already past due in delivering on our value. We should not let another 100 days go by without changing that. Our seat is there, it is ours for the taking.

If I were to wish for anything I should not wish for wealth and power, but for the passionate sense of what can be, for the eye, which, ever young and ardent, sees the possible. Pleasure disappoints, possibility never. And what wine is so sparkling, what so fragrant, what so intoxicating as possibility?

Søren Kierkegaard, Either/Or

References

Berner, R. My Year at Wal-Mart: How Marketing Whiz Julie Roehm Suffered a Spectacular Fall in 10 Short Months." *Business Week*, People/Ousters, February 12, 2007, pp. 70–74.

Bradt, G., Check, J., and Pedraza, J. *New Leaders 100 Day Action Plan.* Hoboken, NJ: Wiley, 2006.

Charan, R. Cited in GO, Development Dimensions International (DDI). Fall 2006 – Vol. 2, No. 2, p. 7.

Conlin, M. "Smashing the Clock: Inside Best Buy's Radical Reshaping of the Workplace." *Business Week*, Special Report, December 11, 2006, pp. 60–68.

Fitz Enz, J. *Human Value Management: The Value Adding Human Resource Management for the 1990s.* San Francisco, CA: Jossey-Bass, 1990.

Fitz Enz, J. *The 8 Practices of Exeptional Companies: How Great Organizations Make the Most of Their Human Assets.* New York, NY: AMACOM, 1997.

Hammonds, K. "Why We Hate HR." *Fast Company*, August, 2005, pp. 41–47.

Huselid, M. A., Becker, B. E., and Beatty, R. W. *The Workforce Scorecard: Managing Human Capital to Execute Strategy.* Boston, MA: Harvard Business School Press, 2005.

John, S. In C. Gorelick, N. Melton and K. April (eds.). *Building a Membership Firm through Practice Communities in Performance through Learning: Knowledge Management in Practice.* Burlington, MA: Elsevier Butterworth-Heineman, 2004.

London, S. "Why Managers Have Little Time for Management Theory." *Financial Times, Business Life*, January 18, 2006, p. 10.

Stern, S. "Human Resources Departments Are Unloved But Not Unnecessary." *Financial Times, Business Life*, April 18, 2006, p. 6.

Ulrich, D. *Human Resources Champions.* Boston, MA: Harvard Business School Press, 1997.

Walker, J. W. *Human Resource Strategy.* New York, NY: McGraw-Hill, 1992.

Watkins, M. *The First 90 Days.* Boston, MA: Harvard Business School Press, 2003.

Zander, R. S., and Zander, B. *The Art of Possibility: Transforming Professional and Personal Life.* Boston, MA: Harvard Business School Press, 2000.

Epilogue

In a career that spans 25 years there have been many moments that stand out. I have experienced some successes, some failures, some learning, some unlearning, some relearning moments that are important to me and, hopefully, to the organizations where I worked. I have worked as an Organization Effectiveness/Executive Education (OE/EE) specialist for some of the world's largest Professional Service, Financial Services, and Pharmaceutical organizations. Each is unique in its strategy, operations, and culture yet each shares similar challenges executing their strategy better than their competition while providing a work environment attractive to an ever-diverse workforce.

There have been a number of recurring themes from employees that capture the essence of the challenges faced by today's organizations:

- We send our people to training programs and little or nothing [different] happens when they return to their jobs.
- Whatever happened to the day's when the individual mattered — when the individual was the most important element of innovative ideas, client service, and building the business — the star system worked out pretty well for a long time.

- Something is not right around here. You know the feeling. It is hard to get work done, to get excited about the work. It just does not feel right here.
- I remember the days when men ran things. We did pretty well for ourselves, our families, and our companies ... everyone benefited.
- Leaders are born. It is a waste of time and money to try to develop them. It cannot be done. Leaders are developed not born so let us get going and develop ours before they leave to go to the competition. This polarized view ensured nothing would be done except debate the issue.
- I can identify great talent after five minutes of interviewing them. I do not need these fancy assessment centers and reports. My gut tells me when a person is right for the job and the company. I have never been wrong.
- Our performance goal setting and performance review process work well. We set them and get going on delivery. Every once in a while we have to give someone a kick to get them on the right track.
- Rewards here are the best. We only reward the best and brightest. I have never heard any complaints so we must be doing things right.
- We do not have time around here for fancy theories — things change too fast here for that stuff. We need to just get on with getting our business done.

These themes were heard 25 years ago, not just today but hopefully not tomorrow. Not every leader articulated them or believes in them. There are leaders, managers, and employees who see different realities or possibilities in their organizations. Individuals and teams who are committed to learning and transferring their learnings to the larger organization are also committed to creating the needed changes in their culture. They seek out kindred spirits who vehemently disagree with most if not all of the themes above.

Early in my career, it became clear that skill building training programs were not meeting the needs of senior management although they almost always were highly rated by participants. In the 1980s and 1990s more and more organizations were developing global strategies and looking for their employees to execute those strategies at higher and higher performance levels. More and more work situations required the formation of diverse teams. No one individual possessed the knowledge and skills to generate and execute solutions to these complex work situations. As the cost of doing business rose and a short-term view of financial performance dominated the business landscape, it became clear to me that individual, team, and organizational level learning needed to be directly connected to the strategy of the organization. Also the speed with which strategy changed became a major challenge for every level of the organization to overcome. Senior Leaders talked frequently about the need for a leader to be able to think on their feet or on the fly. These capabilities were in very short supply then as well as now. Simulations were often built into training programs. These early simulations used fictitious companies. Material about the culture of the organization was sparse, i.e. one or two paragraphs or non-existent. Financial decision-making was heavily emphasized to the exclusion of all other organizational factors. It became clear that even more sophisticated and high impact training experiences would not be sufficient to meet the competitive challenges of 21st century organizations. I found the prevailing wisdom of the day, i.e. learning and transfer was looked at as the outcome of training programs. I came to understand that learning and transfer had to be deeply embedded in the performance management process through goal setting and the performance coaching that should take place throughout the year. It was here that you could see the transfer of all individual and team development efforts and their impact on the organization's strategy execution plans. It was here that you could observe the cultural enablers or impediments to applying learning and leading necessary change.

The 21st century has brought additional challenges to organizations as well as to the OE/EE specialists. Organizations are fighting global competition which makes economic performance difficult. In addition, today's organization is expected to be a good corporate citizen regarding its environmental impact and social responsibility. An organization, if it is to succeed in this environment must be at the top of its strategy execution game. Every individual and team must know/understand the strategy relevant to their area and be able to set goals and actions that deliver results above expectations. They must also be aware of changes in the strategy frequently due to strategic learning and then take the initiative in leading necessary change to strategy, structure, operations, and/or culture. In addition, the learnings must be understood in the context of the strategy execution efforts and acted on the organizational level. As past chairman of Hewlett Packard, Lew Platt, publically stated a number of times "I wish we knew what we know at HP". Under Mark Hurd's leadership HP has regained its number 1 position in the very competitive personal computer (PC) business. The marketing team with the design team focused on building not a commodity PC but one that connected to a purchaser's needs and wants, i.e. their identity as it relates to a pc in their life. Hurd also globalized the marketing strategy developed in the US throughout the world with little or no changes other than language. APC as well became very adept at a one-look product strategy throughout the world utilizing the strategic learnings from the country marketing teams. In both cases the organization was able to make the necessary changes to their organizations strategy, structure, operating processes, and/or culture in time to make a difference in their performance level. They rejected complicated frameworks or theories for the problem at hand. They were able to match the framework and theory needed to know exactly what was required to solve the immediate problem. Kotter almost 20 years ago in his book "Corporate Culture and Performance" noted that companies that understood the culture needed in their industry to succeed and could create that culture in their own organization had superior economic returns over their competition. I believe the same to be true for strategic learning and leading change, i.e. those organizations that can match the learning and change theory to their problem situation will be the winners in their industry space. Recently Apple released the eagerly awaited iPhone. Jobs, Apples CEO, was publically proud of the truly proprietary system characteristics of the phone. Its hardware and the single carrier choice (AT&T) would give Apple a long-term competitive advantage over its competitors. Within hours hackers had figured a way for phone customers to use other carriers. Within days unauthorized phones were available from counterfeiters. The Apple strategy team utilized a few "influentials' to sort out the learnings and make necessary changes. Their success at knowing how to do this is clear in their financial results as well as non-financial measures such as innovation capability and speed of implementing change. Ford presents a very different picture and level of capability to use strategic learning and leading change principles/processes. For well over a decade, Ford has known it needs major change to its strategy, structure, operating processes, and culture. Yet in spite of it knowing this, they have been unable to make the changes necessary for their long-term survival. Perhaps Mullaly, an out of industry executive brought in to save Ford, will be able to more closely match the strategic learning and change framework to Ford and to their problems. In the final analysis for me, its leaderships understanding their organization at its deepest level — its culture — that will determine whether learnings are discussed, reflected on, and then acted on. Finally, Google has recently announced a new strategic direction. The "Google Cloud" strategy will open up the heretofore secret Google computing and data to outsiders. The intent is to put this enormous data and computing power into the hands of many who will learn and generate new solutions to problems. In my mind Google is making strategic learning and leading change the essence of its strategy and not an outcome of its strategy execution efforts. I am reminded of

Albert Einstein's view of theory and problem-solving. He believed that all theories should be a simple as possible to solve the problem at hand but no simpler than needed. Solutions need leaders to implement. Time will tell if Google can field the leadership cadre with the skills to successfully maximize this bold new strategic direction. The HR function should be leading their company's Strategic Learning and Leading Change efforts and not just facilitating or in the worst cases blocking these processes.

I sensed something was very different about APC. They were committed to building a global team-based organization in an industry that was known for its country siloed approach to strategy, operations, and culture. There was excitement and passion in the air. You could feel it. There was also a realism expressed that the challenges would be very difficult and failure was a very possible outcome and success very unlikely. Not cynicism but healthy skepticism. In hearing their excitement and passion, I had to join even though I had spent almost 20 years in professional and financial services organizations. I heard all the themes described above in some manner or form. The challenges for the senior leadership and employees were not much different than any other group of people in any other organization. Nor were the recruiting, performance management/rewards, talent management, and leadership development strategies and processes very different. The difference would be in the way the Top 200 leaders created trust in the proposed strategy, operations, and culture. Time after time they extended their trust to their employees before they asked to be trusted. This led to an enormous amount of employee empowerment. The EC modeled the way for the Top 200 by trusting them first before asking to be trusted. I am reminded of a dear departed colleague, Bob Schachat, who was always fond of saying "Trust is like a butterfly, capricious and delicate. To capture a butterfly one has to use a soft net and a gentle touch". Not behaviors you often find in today's organizations. The EC and the Top 200 used Bob's recommendation by almost always approving the recommendations of the Action Learning Teams that were formed around the pressing strategy, operations, and culture issues facing APC. In addition to trust, a primary difference in the way APC built its new organization was in applying strategic learning and simultaneously changing recruiting, performance management/rewards, talent management, and leadership development strategies and processes over very short periods of time — often in 100 days or less.

APC had a dream as I did when I joined them in 2001. APC was acquired in 2004 before it could realize its dream fully. All of us who were part of the dream could relate to the boy below.

"My heart is afraid it will have to suffer" — the boy said to the Alchemist. "Tell your heart that the fear of suffering is worse than the suffering itself ... and that no heart has ever suffered when it goes in search of its dreams". Paulo Coelho, The Alchemist, 1993.

Each of us who were part of the APC dream is better for it. When I hear people talk of the falling out of grace of the Org Effectiveness function with many senior business leaders, I say to them what the Alchemist said to the boy. I would also add that you should provide management and employees with effective recruiting, performance management/rewards, talent management, and leadership development strategies and processes. Make needed changes quickly utilizing a 100 Day approach and simultaneously to all people processes affected by the changes. Provide management with easy to use/ understand reports on employee engagement and energy levels and the state of the leadership pipeline. This pipeline is critical to sustain high levels of performance as well as developing the future leaders who will move the organization to new heights of innovation, performance, and service to the communities they operate in.

Perhaps the most exciting area to design and implement in today's organization is that of communities of practice. Community makes each person feel part of something much larger than themselves. It adds purpose to their work and to their lives. Community also provides an environment for the organizations identity to be understood, for strategic learning to flourish and for needed changes to be implemented. I believe there has never been a better time to be an Organizational Effectiveness/Executive Education practitioner. The challenges facing all organizations irrespective of size, industry, or location need this expertise. Don Quixote, Kierkegaard, and Coelho, feed our spirit and free us to dream about how our organizations can be better places to work and spend our lives. Strategic learning and leading change bring these dreams into reality. We can create and sustain organizations that are immensely profitable, socially and environmentally responsible, and provide enriching/exciting community like work places for all employees. There is nothing more powerful and satisfying than enabling others to learn, reflect, change, and lead others in the same pursuit. As I noted in the acknowledgements practitioners like Michelle Limantour, Anika Gakovic, and Amy Bladden give strength to my soul that this generation of culture change agents are committed to making organizations more effective and human than any we have seen to date. I remind them to be technically prepared for their work but not to forget the life's lessons taught to us by Quixote, Kierkegaard, and Coello. Paolo Friere was fond of saying "We make the road by walking". My generation of practitioners has carved out the roadway. It will be the new generation's role to pave it for long-term sustained use. I wish them and all who follow god speed.

Index

For Product Safety Concerns and Information please contact our
EU representative GPSR@taylorandfrancis.com Taylor & Francis
Verlag GmbH, Kaufingerstraße 24, 80331 München, Germany